LIVING WITH
YOUR TEENAGER

A Guide for Jewish Parents

by SIMON GLUSTROM

New York

BLOCH PUBLISHING COMPANY

1961

TO MY PARENTS

IDA AND SOLOMON GLUSTROM

WHO HAVE IMPARTED SO MUCH WISDOM

TO THEIR OWN FOUR CHILDREN

Acknowledgments

I am grateful to the following for their help:

Dr. Morton Siegel, Rabbi Mordecai Waxman, Mr. Zalmen Slesinger, and Mr. Roland Burdick, all of whom read the manuscript and offered many valuable suggestions.

Mrs. Alfred Rosenfarb, my secretary, who typed and prepared the manuscript for publication.

Mr. Allan Angoff, who painstakingly read the manuscript and helped prepare it for publication.

The members of the Fair Lawn Jewish Center and their sensitive youngsters who provided so much of the motivation to undertake the writing of this book.

S. G.

Contents

CONTENTS

Preface

"Children now love luxury, they have no manners.
They show contempt for authority, are disrespectful to
their elders and love to chatter instead of exercise. . . .
They contradict their parents, misbehave before company, gobble up dainties at the table, cross their legs and
tyrannize their teachers."

This is not a quotation from a modern parents' magazine; it is Socrates some two thousand years ago lamenting
the behavior of children he could not understand.

We parents continue to complain about the unusual habits
of our young people today. We cannot understand why they
must learn the hard way when by simply heeding their elders
they can avoid trouble. But all healthy human beings learn
by themselves, by trial and error, disregarding more often
than not the advice and wisdom of others. The road to
maturity demands both the process of adaptation *and* rejection.

Adolescent problems have appeared throughout history
among all peoples in all parts of the world. However, the
nature and intensity of the problems have varied, as they

do now, because of social, economic, and religious factors.

Nevertheless, the physical and emotional changes that take place in the transitional stage of adolescence are reflected in new and apparently strange modes of behavior regardless of the milieu in which the child has grown.

Parents of teenagers who have forgotten their own problems in adolescence frequently feel victimized by their loss of authority. They are consoled in some measure by the knowledge that their problems are not at all unique and that teachers and youth leaders who have made a career of guiding young people frequently do not attain successful results.

Parents have for the most part become excessively dependent on the professionals, as if those professionals possess a magical formula for solving teenage problems. But those who have worked most successfully with teenagers emphasize they cannot take the place of parents. For this reason we find that more counsellors today tend to work with the family unit and not merely with the disturbed child.

In this volume I have assumed that parents are capable of undertaking the major responsibility of guiding their own adolescent children and dealing constructively with their problems. Just as parents should continue to develop wholesome attitudes in their children's grooming and eating habits through the period of adolescence, so must they help build positive attitudes toward religious, ethical, and social problems.

We cannot be expected to know all the answers to the complex questions of adolescence, nor to possess the academic and practical background in psychology and religion to better guide the teenager. Indeed, relatively few professionals have this training and experience. However, by sharpening our own interest and curiosity in these areas and by applying common sense based on workaday experience and insight as parents, we can help our youngsters substantially with some of their recurring problems.

I have very deliberately addressed this book to the many Jewish parents who seek direction in dealing with the religious, ethical, and social problems peculiar to our Jewish youth. In recent years there have been some excellent informative books for the Jewish teenagers themselves, but there has been almost no literature directed exclusively to the parents of these Jewish teenagers. The few pamphlets available, along with isolated articles in magazines and anthologies, are extremely helpful to the researcher and the specialist, but the fact is most parents do not know how to seek out this scattered material, and would find much of it too academic or too advanced for the lay reader.

Though the material in this book is simple enough to be understood by many teenagers, it is not directed primarily to them. I am more concerned with the parents' developing a wholesome approach to Jewish problems which will inevitably redound to the benefit of their children.

S. G.

Fair Lawn, New Jersey

Part I
Our Teenager's World

1

Understanding the Adolescent

The phenomenal increase in our teenage population is sufficient reason to seek more information about it. Between 1958 and 1960 the number of children reaching age thirteen rose forty per cent. By 1965 there will be a thirty-five per cent increase in the fourteen to seventeen age group. The total population growth, it should be noted, is two per cent a year. However, there is much more about the teenager than his numerical increase to warrant our attention. Social workers, psychiatrists, teachers, clergymen—in fact, most professionals who must work with them insist we must better understand their erratic behavior patterns. Enlightened parents have long asked for guidance in controlling and channeling the restiveness and rebelliousness, the moodiness and unresponsiveness, of their once docile child.

Authoritative opinions about the causes of the conspicuous changes in growing children are numerous and varied. One student of adolescent behavior calls the period of adolescence the "second birth," suggesting that the changes that have taken place in the "new being" are almost as crucial as the differences that occur between the prenatal and infant stages.

Another authority stresses that adolescence represents a stage in which emotional development has lagged behind physical development. Thus, we have a child and an adult combined in one person, but with bitter competition and serious conflict between the two. "The boy or girl enters adolescence with a child's adjustment to the world," says Louella Cole, "but no matter how perfect his emotional and social adaptation may be, it is not suitable for adult life." [1]

Drs. H. H. Remmers and D. H. Radler put it this way in their book, *The American Teenager:* "On the way to adult poise, Jerry and Susie pass through awkward misery. Their erstwhile smooth and working bodies turn into gangly, ill-coordinated machines. Their noses, growing faster than the rest of their bodies, threaten to topple them forward. Their rosy skins, glowing just a moment ago with the bloom of childhood, now look to them like some nightmare field of black pits and erupting volcanoes."

These physical changes are so sudden and obvious that the adolescent becomes more acutely aware of them than at other stages in his life. Only during the profound transition from middle age to old age is there a comparable change. Although the observer can see more growth and maturation in the child during the pre-adolescent period than during adolescence, the pre-adolescent is not capable of as much self-observation. This awareness of his physical changes causes considerable unhappiness for the teenager. He worries about the disparity between his physical ability and his ideal of what that ability should be, and he finds himself wanting in physical strength and a pleasing appearance. He finds that the once well-oiled machine lacks coordination, and he tends to react with fright and loss of self-esteem. These negative reactions affect him physically, causing more awkwardness and greater physical

[1] Cole, Louella. *Psychology of Adolescence.* Rinehart & Co. N. Y. 1954.

discomfort. Feelings of bashfulness and shame often develop. He wishes that no one would look at him. He desires invisibility. Realizing that he must be seen, he often compensates for his feelings by acts of rudeness and other anti-social attitudes in the hope that he can drive away onlookers. At times he accepts the fact that he appears awkward and flaunts it in order to evoke laughter, or, in order to find consolation, he may invite sympathy by displaying constant unhappiness.

Although we cannot change physical characteristics, we can influence the child's attitudes toward them. One thing that obviously should be avoided is the practice of calling attention to these changes in a degrading and sarcastic manner. Some well-meaning but tactless adults actually create more self-consciousness about appearance in the very child they are trying to help. For example, to be repeatedly scolded for poor posture as something wrong makes a child feel guilty, just as he may come to think of face pimples as revealing a sinful act committed in secrecy.

However, any attempt to generalize about the behavior patterns of adolescents has its limitations. In addition to the vast changes of attitude and behavior that take place between, say, the ages of thirteen and seventeen, one finds in children of similar ages completely different responses.[2] Some are obviously well-adjusted, of cheerful mind, and are excellently coordinated physically. Others are dejected and moody, and retire into convenient shells of escape. There are those who at

---

[2] Adolescence has been generally broken down into the following stages:
a) Early adolescence, 13 to 15 years (girls); 15 to 17 years (boys)
b) Middle adolescence, 15 to 18 years (girls); 17 to 19 years (boys)
c) Late adolescence, 18 to 21 years (girls); 19 to 21 years (boys)

It is interesting to note that the period of adolescence never lasted as long in the past as it does in our society. In early America children completed their schooling at the age of twelve or thirteen and went immediately to work. They married early and supported a family at the age of eighteen or nineteen.

the age of fourteen and fifteen sense a deep feeling of faith in God and there are others who become cynics and skeptics. Adolescents differ greatly in their degree of self-awareness. One child knows precisely what he wants, while another is hesitant and halting about his wishes and convictions. He may pretend to be following his own convictions when he is blindly following what others say he should do. One adolescent may be adept at sizing up his abilities and qualities; another may be utterly ignorant of his strength. One adolescent may permit his feelings to well up within him and recognize them for what they are, accepting himself as one who has his periods of anger, fear, and depression. Another, retreating from his emotions, may be unable to understand his uneasiness and the blue days which descend upon him to further bewilder and depress him.

If anything close to a generalization can be made about the adolescent, it is that friendship means more to him now than at any other stage in life. He wants to be counted in socially. His most immediate problem is group approval and acceptance, and so intense is this urge that means become less important than ends in attaining this goal. In fact, he is more interested in seeking the approbation of friends than of parents or teachers.

This need for group approval is clearly evident in almost everything the youngster does. He wants to dress like his friends; he wants to talk the way they do. His haircut has to be exactly the same. He demands the same privileges and liberties that his companions have. He demands the same allowance, likes the same type of music, dances the same way, enjoys the same interests, takes on the same prejudices and the same fears.

This drive toward conformity in adolescence has its dangerous implications because it involves a kind of self-surrender. But it is also part of a normal and realistic adjustment to life. Through observing and imitating the conduct of others, the young person discovers the humanity he shares with them. As he moves out from his limited world to the world of his companions, he needs to notice what others do and say, what are their rules and their values. For the sake of good will, even the very individualistic child will not deviate too obviously from the customs of the crowd.

This herd instinct serves yet another useful purpose. It gives each member of the group equal importance and reinforces his self-confidence with the knowledge that he is accepted by his peers even if the adult world seems to reject him. He finds comfort in learning that he is not alone in his rebelliousness; the whole group shares his feelings of guilt, and so lessens them.

The physical changes in maturing teenagers is accompanied by the discovery of newly-found strength and boundless energy which must find an outlet. For many, dancing (more often of the visceral type) and athletics satisfy their physical needs. Those who do not consume their energies in normal healthy activity sometimes develop a destructiveness which is vented on people and property. Juvenile delinquency may be traced in part to this misdirected energy which, if properly channeled, could be directed to more creative and productive goals.

Frequently this abundance of energy which fails to find a sufficient outlet creates the boredom of which many teenagers complain. They cannot find enough activity to sustain their interest and consume their time. Middle-aged people are happy if they can muster enough energy to carry them through their normal daily routines. Not so the teenager who is a virtual storehouse of energy.

Adolescent boredom has also been linked with anxiety and

resentment, due in part to the "barrenness of his environment." It may result from feeling ill at ease when left to himself as though he were unable to enjoy or even endure his own company in solitude.[3]

The feeling of rootlessness and loneliness is not exclusively a teenage problem. It is a general malady of an age in which the rapid pace of living and the fear of mass destruction have taken their toll. But this feeling is especially prevalent during adolescence. It is not too difficult to understand why this period of transition, when one is neither child nor adult, is fraught with these feelings. All human beings seek the comfort of identification within a particular group and the security of knowing exactly where they belong and how they fit into the fabric of society; but when body, mind and emotions change with such rapidity, feelings of uncertainty regarding their status prevail.

Then there are the external factors that intensify this problem of rootlessness. Today's teenagers were born during or after World War II. They have lived through the Korean War and the continuing tensions between East and West. They are aware that they will be called to serve in the armed forces for a few years. They are frequently uncertain about their careers, knowing that their chances for admittance into the college of their choice are becoming increasingly narrowed. They must be prepared to limit their planning for the future.

The emotional problems of adolescence are compounded by the fact that the older generation doesn't know how to regard the adolescent and how to react to his specific problems. Should he be treated like the child he once was, or like the adult he thinks he is? If he is spoken to in the same manner as one speaks to a ten-year-old, he may rebel or, at

[3] Jersild, Arthur T. *The Psychology of Adolescence,* Macmillan, N. Y. 1957.

best, ignore the request of the adult. And to deal with him as one would a mature person means giving him responsibility which he may not be prepared to undertake.

Parents often seem exasperated by the listlessness of their child, their inability to interest him in things that are happening outside of his little world. But when a child's energies are already sapped by the problem of physical growth, by social activities in and out of school, by decisions which will affect his entire life; when he is bewildered by the shifting attitude of teachers and parents and society in general, all of whom doubt him and his behavior; when he is bewildered by a complex and rapidly changing civilization into which he must soon adjust, it is not difficult to understand why he has little desire left to assume other responsibilities and interests.

Frequently parents complain that their children think of them as old-fashioned, out of step with contemporary fashion. Naturally, mother and father are offended when they consciously strive so hard to keep up with these trends. When the child claims his parents are old-fashioned, he is denying they are alert and progressive. The props are completely knocked out from under them. But the teenager seems to have something particular in mind which the parents may fail to understand. His criticism will remain unchanged however modern the parents are. He expects their unqualified acceptance of his adolescent world; he would like to have them feel the same great urgency about his needs as he does, which may have been possible when they were teenagers, but which is now impracticable. But the teenager will learn this only when he has his own family and adult responsibilities.

Though tensions are common, they are by no means inevitable. Parents of pre-adolescents need not feel that they *must* brace themselves for a trying and exhausting period, just as the childhood stages of stealing or lying may never appear and need not be anticipated. Although these unsocial acts are not at all abnormal, the young child may have had little reason to indulge in them. Very often, the more turbulent the childhood, the calmer the adolescence, for much of the emotional upheaval has resolved itself by the time adolescence sets in.

Anthropologists have found that in some primitive cultures the average teenager is a happy, efficient, well-adjusted member of his society.[4] Parental expectation of crises may actually invite particular behavior problems that might have been avoided had they been handled more casually. Incipient problems are often brought to full bloom unnecessarily by the exaggerated build-up that parents give them.

Researchers tend to ignore the joys of the adolescent who often experiences pleasure—as when he is cordially accepted by his own age group; when he succeeds in ventures in and out of school; when he is respected for his maturity and appreciated as one who not only can carry added responsibilities but can also be granted new privileges, or when he begins to discover the talents and abilities that emerge during adolescence.

Perhaps we err in yet another way. We are no longer inclined to think of teenagers as just young people in transition between childhood and adulthood. We have come to regard them as a large pressure group with their powerful lobbying influence on our culture. It is altogether possible we have become obsessed with classifications. In the past we spoke of "youngsters," "schoolboys" and "schoolgirls," but we did not find teenagers as strictly defined as they are today. Classification may often help us in our understanding of people, but sometimes it creates a stigma, particularly among oversensi-

---

[4] Meade, M. *Coming of Age in Samoa.* New York: Morrow, 1928.

tive young people. Adolescents know that they are a problem group and the subject of considerable discussion by their parents, sociologists, psychiatrists, and others. They are dissatisfied with themselves for not living up to the standards which others expect of them. But it becomes quite simple to rationalize one's behavior after he has been marked as a member of a problem group.

The startling rise of juvenile delinquency during the recent past is sufficient cause for alarm. Nevertheless, adults should be particularly careful not to condemn a whole society of teenagers because of the destructiveness of what is a fractional minority within the teenage group. The younger generation is not lost and doomed to certain self-destruction. Many of today's critics were themselves once given up, along with their whole generation, as lost also for rebelling against the accepted mores of an earlier America. But they resolved many of their more acute emotional problems, and with maturity went on to gain for themselves a more or less respectable position in society.

In the face of all these possible tensions and crises, the adolescent years often give parents sufficient reason for encouragement and pride in their children. They are heartened by the sharpened curiosity of the child, his ability to discuss and debate on a stimulating level. They are impressed with the child's desire to earn money after school hours or during vacation, with his display of ingenuity and his ability in particular fields of endeavor. The teens become in some instances the years of career planning when parents enthusiastically explore the many possibilities of the future with the child.

In general, most parents will affirm that despite the problems attending these years, the household is filled with constant excitement. Elderly people, reflecting on those years that have passed, nostalgically recall that the very period when their own homes reached the peak of excitement were the years when their children were in their teens.

The American teenager has therefore very understandably been called the most exasperating, the most unpredictable and, perhaps most important, the most inspiring citizen in America.

2

The Teenager Faces Religion

We cannot predict a young person's reaction to religion once he becomes involved in the complex of adolescent living. His religious views are as subject to rapid change and are as unpredictable as his height and weight. Those parents who anticipate the novelty of surprise are not likely to be disappointed.

What has been said about the difficulty of generalizing about the teenager's reactions is equally applicable to his religion. To some teenagers religion had little meaning before that age and has had even less since. Others find meaning in religion for the first time during these years. A multitude of biographies and autobiographies reveals that religious experience in adolescence may be profound, ranging from ecstatic joy to despair and despondency.

Religious attitudes emerge from a variety of factors:

A—*Attitude toward parents:*

A young person's total personality and his upbringing until the time he attains adolescence will have an important bearing on his religious views during the adolescent years.

To realize the meaning of love, kindness, and forbearance,

as emphasized in religion, the teenager must draw primarily upon his own experience with loving parents. To have realized the meaning of faith, he should have been capable of experiencing something of the meaning of faith and trust at an early age. When his parents' ethical and religious ideals are grounded in a capacity to give and receive love, the child will have an opportunity prior to the teenage years to grow into convictions that become an inextricable part of his own life.

If father has been a strict disciplinarian, unyielding to the needs of the child, then it is altogether possible that the adolescent, nursing the wounds of resentment and animosity, will adopt a negative conception of God. Sometimes he may reject the rigid parent, and in so doing will also want to sever himself from everything the parent deems sacred, including his religion.

B—*The religious attitudes of friends:*

If attendance at and an interest in religious services, and discussions about religion are common among his group of friends, then the teenager is likely to gravitate to these activities to strengthen his ties with them. He wants to share the interests of his companions and thus to become an integral part of the group. I know well several children who without any previous Jewish background or home stimulus became synagogue-conscious because their close friends were religious-minded teenagers who accepted the synagogue in their daily lives.

C—*The influence of heroic figures:*

Young people have always worshipped heroes. Adolescents in every culture have sought to pattern their lives after strong personalities. Socrates was a hero to thousands of youths in his day. (In fact, he was condemned to death on the accusation that he corrupted the youth of Athens.) Martin Buber was regarded as a hero to a large segment of Jewish youth in pre-Nazi Germany. Occasionally, a folk hero who is long dead or who may never have lived continues to command the attention of young people. This search for an ideal type outside the family occurs in the development of every individual and is part of the process of growing up.

These heroic figures are important forces in the life of the teenager and in his ambitions and later development. Witness the fan club craze in the United States and the assured financial success of singers who can sufficiently impress teenagers to buy their records. It is fair to say that today teenagers are influencing the success or failure of popular artists who seek a mass national audience more than any other group of Americans.

These teenagers are vitally interested in the private lives, the opinions and activities of their heroic figures. If religion means a great deal to an athletic coach who is outspoken in his religious views, he can have a decided effect on the enchanted youngster and his religious outlook. Even the clergyman, who dedicates his life's work to religion, is not as influential as the teenage hero with a positive religious outlook.

D—*The influence of other interests and sentiments:*

The youth who has fallen in love may find that the exaltation of romance is in some ways similar to a religious experience. His romantic ideals and ambitions may very well blend with a religious desire to embrace the whole universe. He sees purpose and meaning in everything. He admires God's creation and is filled with faith and optimism. He sees his individual role in the world more clearly than ever before and is grateful to God for his good fortune. Conversely, a bitter experience with a boy or girl friend may shatter one's enthusiasm for religion.

Appreciation for the aesthetic may also influence teenage

religious feeling. Those for whom art has become an adolescent passion often experience deep religious sentiments. Gordon Allport has indicated that "youth often finds that religion is only art transposed to a higher key, for like art it seeks to unify and harmonize that with which it deals."

E—*The influence of earlier religious training:*

The religious views of teenagers are greatly influenced by the extent and quality of their religious education during the formative years. What Lenin said about the lasting influence of socialism on the minds of those indoctrinated in their youth holds true for religion.

Much depends on the way in which the God concept was presented to him in his very early years. Now that he is introduced to the study of the sciences, is he forced to renounce his previous views about God or can he merely add to these simple but sound concepts of his childhood? Was God pictured as a man? Were angels and Satan presented literally? Were miracles taught to be accepted unequivocally? If so, then the chances of the adolescent retaining a healthy respect for religion are greatly impaired. But if his teacher or parent had kept in mind that some religious concepts need never be rejected or accepted, but rather grown into with maturity, then he was wisely preparing the child for the progressive strengthening of his religious outlook in the adult years.

Despite the personal problems and the religious doubts that prevail among adolescents, religion can play a most vital role in their personal lives during these critical years. Teenagers, especially the older ones, are intensely concerned with the destiny of man and the meaning of life. Surveys conducted among them have revealed that their most frequently mentioned wishes were for "peace," [1] "to be better,"

[1] ". . . . The psychological origins of the adolescent's social idealism lie in his yearning for peace within himself, and this in turn arises as a reaction

"to be nicer," "for happiness" (for themselves and others), and "for betterment of society." In addition to these desires, many girls expressed the wish to be devoted wives and mothers. It is most significant that all of these expressed ideals are within the purview of religion.

This problem of self acceptance, which is prevalent among a large segment of our youth, is also a religious problem, though not exclusively. The void that comes with loneliness and rootlessness, alluded to in the previous chapter, can often be replaced by a sense of the inner, all-pervading security stressed by teachers of religion. When people, no matter what their age, can feel at home in the world and can further feel that they have an important role to play, then much that stands in the way of self esteem is removed. A firm belief in God as an ally and partner can greatly enhance the feeling of at-homeness in the world.

Religion can play still another role in helping the teenager. In the process of coming into one's own, a young person is likely to find the going painful at times. In discovering his limitations and shortcomings, he is prone to suffer, and in the process of freeing himself of self-deception he is bound to undergo periods of extreme discomfort. Furthermore, to achieve true maturity he must take risks and bear up under the pain of disappointment that occurs when he fails in some of his ventures.

Religion can help the young person realize that suffering is not always tragic. The history of religion has taught us that almost all great men who tried to live according to their religious ideals met with adversity and endured sorrow. The

to the inner struggle that erupts at puberty. The adolescent tends to project his feelings of helplessness and turmoil onto the outer world, so that his yearning for inner peace may take the form of a wish for world peace."

Linn, Louis, M. D., and Schwartz, Leo, *Psychiatry and Religious Experience.* Random House, N. Y. 1958.

great prophets were confronted with failure and disappointment precisely because they were venturesome. But without
struggle they never would have attained greatness.

Serious religious doubts are often experienced for the first
time during the stress of puberty. At this period of development the youth is no longer content to let his parents think
for him. He has developed a more critical and searching mind
and no longer follows unquestioningly their religious pattern.
Although the transformation is often imperceptible, more often there is a period of open rebellion which may take on
varied forms. Occasionally he will attend a different place of
worship than his parents. Or he may refuse to participate in
any form of religious observance, or will gravitate toward
non-observant friends with whom he feels more comfortable.
Occasionally rebellion is not related to intellectual doubt, but
springs from emotional factors: rejection, or feelings of guilt
and shame due to sex conflicts.

What are some of the criticisms and doubts that teenagers
have expressed about religion?

1—They see little or no relationship between religion and
the practical problems of their everyday lives. At best it appears to be outmoded and archaic, out of step with the needs
of most people in the modern world.

Many young people are obsessed with things modern. The
last word in fashion, the latest model automobile, the newest
scientific discovery—all represent progress. The old becomes
synonomous with the obsolete. One teenager characteristic-
ally expressed to me his disinterest in religion with the question, "Why do you have to live with a Model-T when you can
afford a Cadillac?" The problem is not confined to young
people. Their parents too are banefully influenced by the
world of motivation research which thrives on the concept
of psychological obsolescence.

2—They become concerned with the chasm between what is preached and practiced. People may come to a service to pray and listen attentively to a sermon, and they will try to impress others with their piety, but they are not really influenced by religion in their daily practices. Many adolescents find this criticism not only among practitioners of religion, but all around them. They react to this discrepancy in government which preaches democracy but fails to practice it; they criticize the school which claims it is concerned with the needs of its students but doesn't take the trouble to inquire into the true nature of those needs. They have difficulty in understanding why one man may be sent to jail for dishonesty, while another may win an honored place in the community because he is shrewd enough to evade the law.

3—They complain that the language of prayer is not relevant to their needs. The prayer book does not read smoothly and cannot be digested as easily as a contemporary piece of literature. They also complain that the service is too long, repetitive, and monotonous. Why can't one fulfill his obligations by reciting a short spontaneous prayer without repeating what others have written?

Similarly, doubts have been expressed about the lack of consideration for individual needs. Typical is this complaint against organized religion: "Why must I be told when to worship? I pray when my spirit is moved, when I see a beautiful rainbow or hear inspiring music. How can I be expected to be in the mood for prayer at a certain time and place on Saturday or Sunday."

4—Religion is anti-scientific and therefore impedes progress. It does not take into account the great advances that have been made in technology and science. Religion concerns itself with conserving old forms and concepts that originated in the pre-scientific era.

Unfortunately, many young people are given the impression that the conflict between religion and science is irreconcilable and that they must choose one or the other. To accept religion *or* reason, as though they were incompatible, is to misunderstand the meaning of both. Yet, this impression is frequently left with them. Usually a teacher with little regard for religion or a clergyman who denies the validity of science reveals something about his own uncertainties and his need to justify himself by putting others in the wrong. The mature scientist is humble and cautious, realizing the immensity of his ignorance. The man with genuine religious faith is likewise hesitant to quarrel with men of science; the more confident he is in his faith, the more he can respect other disciplines.

This source of skepticism is not as widespread as one would expect. Gesell [2] reports that more skepticism concerning God is expressed at thirteen than at any other age in adolescence. "Most of our subjects express some degree of disbelief in God. The majority are dubious, some are 'uninterested,' and the rest flatly disbelieve." On the other hand, at sixteen there is greater belief in a divinity than at any preceding age. The great majority of the group believe in some sort of power greater than man. Certainly the sixteen-year-old has studied more science than the thirteen-year-old!

Perhaps the answer to the paradox lies in the important transition that has already been made at sixteen. The Deity is now conceived as less human-like in form than at an earlier age. God is now looked upon as an intangible Being or something eternal, and therefore more acceptable.

5—The conventional ideas about God's omnipotence, the

[2] Gesell, Arnold, Ilg, Frances L., and Ames, Louis B., *Youth, The Years From Ten to Sixteen.* New York: Harper, 1956.

miracles recorded in the Bible, the belief in immortality, the existence of a soul are called into question.

6—Religion in his mind is largely associated with "thou shalt" and "thou shalt not," which are commands similar to those the teenager hears all day from authorities in the home and at school. It is painful enough to be told what to do by parents and teachers; why must he accept still another authority which inhibits him even more? The teenager tends to associate the church and synagogue with "purity" which he identifies with "prudery," and above all he want to avoid being stigmatized as a prude, for that would make him lose status among friends.

The aforementioned doubts and criticisms are also experienced by adults of all ages; the clergyman addresses himself to these problems regularly throughout his career. However, during the adolescent years the seed of skepticism is sown, takes root, and becomes so deeply imbedded that it occasionally remains with a man for the remainder of his life.

Though skepticism is widespread among the teenage set, the results do not as a rule create a religious upheaval. The average teenager does not seek the added discomfort of questioning the integrity of those who have taught him and in whom he has placed his trust. The process of doubting is frequently too painful. To question one's cherished beliefs is disturbing at any stage in life and especially during adolescence, when comfort and security are most urgently sought.

3

The Jewish
Teenager

When a well-known public speaker commented, "Jews are like everyone else but even more so," he had in mind the particular problems in being Jewish along with all the other human problems of all people. The Jewish adolescent is no exception. He struggles continually with the problems of acceptance and Jewish identity in a non-Jewish society. At times he is self-conscious upon hearing the word "Jew" or a Jewish name mentioned publicly. He senses his minority status and is aware for the first time of the implications of anti-Semitism. He hears that Jews are not welcome everywhere, that their opportunities are more limited than those of his Christian friends, that he has even less chance of admission to some colleges than some friends who are not as qualified as he is.

He finds out during these years that there are dating problems. His parents are uneasy about his going out occasionally with a non-Jewish girl friend. They fear the possibility of a more serious relationship that may culminate in marriage.

The teenager cannot quite grasp it all. He has been taught tolerance and understanding all these years, and now it seems his parents didn't mean a thing they were saying. His rabbi appears narrow despite his education and general liberal viewpoint because he too advises young Jewish people to date within their own religious group. The teenager may then begin to look upon Jews as clannish and on all religion as a divisive force in society.

Much of his difficulty may stem from an inadequate Jewish education which may have begun late, only to be ended at the age of thirteen. During those all-too-few years, he was drilled in elementary Hebrew and presented with a smattering of history about Jewish holidays and customs. Just at the age when he might have begun to appreciate the exalted values of his tradition, his Jewish education was ended to ease his overcrowded social and school schedule.

Why a Jew should be so anxious to preserve his heritage at great personal expense is difficult to fathom. He feels that he has outgrown Judaism and surpassed those who take it so seriously. He may admit that he will find need for it in the future, perhaps when he is well on in years, but not now. Besides, Judaism demands more than he is willing to give up for it. Were he committed to it, it would interfere with the school dances that invariably seem to be set for Friday evenings. He would have to pass up basketball practice Saturday mornings. He might also fall behind in his studies, for observance of Jewish holidays requires considerable absence from school, thus possibly hindering scholastic achievement. "After all," he reasons, "we are living in a Christian country; why fight against it?" He is satisfied to be treated with tolerance by the non-Jews.

One finds among Jewish adolescents the familiar tendency to criticize the entire structure of Judaism because of a single practice or concept which offends them. For example, they will attack Jewish beliefs and practices as a whole because they are offended by the Chosen People concept which many are aware is fundamental to traditional Judaism. In a society which extolls equalitarianism as part of the American way of life, they are sensitive to the possibility of being called undemocratic and snobbish. Bernard Rosen in his study of three adolescent Jewish groups [1] found that 54 per cent of the respondents agreed with this statement: "It is undemocratic for Jews to consider themselves a Chosen People."

Likewise, they tend to show apathy toward the whole complex of Judaism because of negative feelings about the dietary laws. Lacking a broad knowledge of Judaism, they will find one or two particular objections sufficient to reject a complete way of life.

Much has been stated in recent years about the phenomenal revival of Judaism in the United States. Whether the present revival is genuine or not will be appraised more authoritatively by future historians. But one condition upon which a true renaissance of Judaism depends has not as yet been met: Jewish teenagers as a whole still resist wholehearted commitment to Jewish life. When confronted with a choice between religious and social activities, they usually choose the latter. Their Jewish reading is negligible. They are reluctant to enter fields of Jewish service, such as Hebrew teaching and Jewish social work. Only a small but dedicated nucleus is unequivocally committed to live an affirmative Jewish life in spite of its demands and the self-discipline it often imposes.

The teenagers who do respond positively to Jewish life are frequently those who are prepared to meet the intellectual challenge their decision presents. They seek an added stimu-

---

[1] *Minority Group in Transition: A Study of Adolescent Religious Conviction and Conduct.* Published in *The Jews,* edited by M. Sklare, Free Press, Glencoe, Ill. (1958).

lus to satisfy their vibrant curiosity and they find in Jewish
thought and history the very challenge they seek. If the general intellectual level of our youth were elevated it might
well have a more salutary effect on their attitudes to Judaism,
a development which could in turn influence the whole
course of American Jewish life in the future.

Many of those boys and girls who have found their religion
a meaningful experience are given little encouragement by
their parents. Sometimes indifferent parents look on aloofly as
children carry out the home observances and attend services
in the synagogue. When children do it themselves, they are
not partaking of the deep family experience Judaism should
mean to parents and children.

Happily, within the past decade or so, synagogues working
in cooperation with their national organizations have begun
to deal with this critical teenage problem. Serious-minded
children have found encouragement and incentive in the
knowledge that they are not alone, that there are others in
the community and in neighboring towns who are impressed
with Jewish life and with whom they can share the experience. It is heartening to observe how imbued these young
people become with their tradition after having attended an
institute or a conference where they have heard and partici-
pated in candid discussions on the value of *mitzvot,* prayer,
or Sabbath observance.

Another important advantage of affiliation with a synagogue
group is the broad scope of its program in many congregations. It helps to combat the "habit of emphatic provincial-
ism," to use a phrase of Professor Harry Overstreet, who has
also remarked, "In most homes, schools, communities, children are encouraged to achieve only a limited provincial
growth beyond ego-centricity."

These synagogue-centered youth organizations stimulate

adolescent responsibility to the Jewish people, to the local and national community, and to the world community. Their programs and projects are frequently devoted to discussions of their moral and financial obligations to cultural institutions, such as the Jewish Theological Seminary of America, the Hebrew Union College—Jewish Institute of Religion, and the Isaac Elchanan Theological Seminary. They also discuss Zionist ideology and the needs of modern Israel, and are encouraged to support the United Jewish Appeal, Bonds for Israel, and the various cultural and religious institutions in Israel.

They also become well acquainted here with the needs of national charities such as American Red Cross and the March of Dimes. United Nations Week and Brotherhood Week are observed along with Jewish events. The more effective youth organizations in the synagogue are beginning to represent a miniature Jewish community in which young people are prepared for mature Jewish living within the American community of tomorrow in which they may live and work as citizens who are also profoundly aware of their particular heritage as Jews.

A survey published in *Jewish Social Studies* (1955), dealing with the attitudes of Jewish adolescents from 200 families in a middle-sized Jewish community toward their religion, concludes that the era of turbulence and instability in American Jewish life appears to have drawn to a close. Three sociologists found, surprisingly enough, that 97 per cent of the adolescents, when asked, "What is a Jew?" answered in terms of religion. Regarding synagogue attendance, there seemed to be no widespread rebellion and little feeling of coercion by traditional parents. Of those adolescents who did attend services, the majority felt that they went voluntarily rather than because of the urgings of their parents.

When asked, "How do you feel about your parents observing these customs?" 83 per cent of the teenagers reacted positively. In fact, 61 per cent of them felt that when they attended the synagogue, they enjoyed the service. Only 11 per cent showed outright negative feelings. Whether these findings indicate a trend is questionable, but they would seem to reveal a modest but heartening departure from the predominant negative or aloof attitudes toward Jewish life during the past decade.

In another survey, however, published by H. H. Remmers and D. H. Radler in their book *The American Teenager,* we must note the less encouraging findings about Jewish teenagers. These social scientists had been polling teenagers for more than fifteen years. Their results are based on the replies of thousands of teenagers from representative areas throughout the country, and they are startling. Jewish teenagers seem to have the most personal problems among the major religious groups. For example, 35 per cent of Protestant and Catholic teenagers worry about "little things," which 54 per cent of the Jewish youngsters worry about; 27 per cent of the Jewish youngsters feel that they do not get enough sleep, while only 15 per cent of the Protestants and 11 per cent of the Catholics feel that way. More Jewish children feel they must always be on the go, and they also admit to more nervousness and loneliness than children in the two other major religious groups.

Regarding their religious practices and beliefs, these were some of the findings:

A—Attend services once a week: 27 per cent Jews; 40 per cent Protestants; 52 per cent Catholics.
Attend few times a year: 31 per cent Jews; 11 per cent Protestants; 5 per cent Catholics.

Practically never: 15 per cent Jews; 5 per cent Protestants; 4 per cent Catholics.

B—"The more I learn about science, the more I doubt religious beliefs."—19 per cent Jews; 13 per cent Protestants; 10 per cent Catholics.

C—"Religious faith is better than logic in solving life's important problems."—23 per cent Jews; 57 per cent Protestants; 63 per cent Catholics.

D—"God controls everything that happens."—31 per cent Jews; 59 per cent Protestants; 69 per cent Catholics.

E—"Men can build a good society everywhere without divine help."—50 per cent Jews; 34 per cent Protestants; 24 per cent Catholics.

F—"My religious beliefs have made me very happy."—5 per cent Jews; 34 per cent Protestants; 46 per cent Catholics.

"Neither happy nor unhappy."—45 per cent Jews; 24 per cent Protestants; 14 per cent Catholics.

G—"God is only a symbol of man's ideals."—27 per cent Jews; 9 per cent Protestants; 5 per cent Catholics.

H—"The one group that can promote peace in the world are religious leaders."—15 per cent Jews; 50 per cent Protestants; 55 per cent Catholics.

"Educators."—50 per cent Jews; 23 per cent Protestants; and 20 per cent Catholics.

I—"My prayers are always answered."—0 per cent Jews; 22 per cent Protestants; 22 per cent Catholics.

"I never say prayers."—15 per cent Jews; 7 per cent Protestants; and 3 per cent Catholics.

These comparative findings seem bleak and discouraging until we consider the comments of another distinguished authority, Dr. Kurt Lewin,[2] who conducted considerable re-

[2] Lewin K., *Resolving Social Conflicts*, Harper & Bros. N. Y. 1948.

search on this problem. Adolescents, he feels, can be reached through the "Interdependence of Fate" concept, i.e., what happens in a particular Jewish community or to an individual Jew, affects Jews everywhere. To understand and accept this concept of interdependence presumes the youngster's desire to see the Jewish people survive as a group.

Keeping this in mind, we might approach the child by bringing up the question of Jewish survival over the centuries. How is such survival possible, we might ask, unless all Jews contribute in some way to that end? And what better way of contributing to that end than by helping now to preserve the ideas, the institutions, and many of the observances which have meant so much in giving the Jews their enduring unity which is one of the wonders of history?

Teenagers may criticize the synagogue service, its lack of appeal, the repetition of prayers, but the encouraging and startling fact remains that only a negligible number wants to see the dissolution of the synagogue. They are conscious of its indispensability to Jewish survival. We may therefore ask the Jewish teenager, "Suppose the survival of the synagogue had depended on *you* in the past five years. Would the doors have been closed or remained open?" This is a valid and meaningful approach to those youngsters who may be confused about their responsibility to the synagogue and to Jewish life in general.

The Jewish child almost invariably reaches a stage where he shows keen sensitivity to Jewish names. He begins to react personally to names in the news. He takes pride in those Jews who are cited for accomplishment and feels something akin to personal injury or shame when he reads about less admirable acts of other Jews. He wonders what the non-Jew may be saying. He likes to read and hear stories about outstanding Jewish personalities in sports, politics, science. The example of these eminent men and women helps to encourage him as he looks to his own future vocation. He reasons that a Jew can still get ahead if he diligently applies himself. Moreover, he feels that these prominent Jews have helped to raise his own status in the eyes of non-Jews.

Keeping this adolescent interest in mind, two vital points can be effectively stressed by parent and educator.

1—What a man becomes is not the result of any one factor. More often than not, one's Jewish heritage helps to influence his makeup. Such men as Herbert Lehman, Albert Einstein, and Sigmund Freud inherited more than biological traits from their parents. They were also influenced by their Jewish predecessors dating back hundreds of years.

There are of course unknown factors which probably have nothing to do with Jewish influence. But the love for learning, the spirit of liberal giving and thinking, the drive against conformity—these are nevertheless but a few specific Jewish traits that still inhere within Jews, although some may be far removed from traditional Judaism. However, we should not think that these outstanding traits will be passed on indefinitely. The future influence of Jewish values will depend largely on our desire to keep the flame of our heritage burning.

2—A person who has self-respect will more probably be respected by others. Those who cannot learn to accept themselves as Jews will likely develop traits of bitterness. Their unhappiness will be displayed in their poor relationship with people, who in turn will look upon them as cynical and uncooperative. Conversely, the person who has resolved the problem of self-acceptance will, because of his more natural attitude, inspire confidence and respect. He will be a happier person for it.

Brief mention has been made of the traditional Jewish love of learning. For centuries, Jewish parents have emphasized scholastic achievement, and in America the emphasis still persists, though in the secular field rather than in the area of Jewish scholarship. The modern Jewish parent is less concerned with scholarly achievement for its own sake, but rather with the opportunities that scholarly achievement makes more probable for gaining entrance into a college of national repute and, later, for success in the business and professional world.

In their anxiety to have their child succeed, parents may unintentionally overrate his mental capacity, transmitting their anxiety to him who, in turn, feels guilty for failing to live up to his parents' expectations. Comparisons are all-too-often drawn with the children of neighbors who are more gifted intellectually, thus adding to the child's lack of self-confidence and self-esteem.

Other anxious parents bent on successful careers for their children show open dissatisfaction with the less lucrative vocations in spite of the child's own leanings. The youngster who is determined to become a teacher, an artist, an actor, or a clerical worker, may find far more satisfaction than the seemingly successful business or professional man whose life's ambition was diminished or destroyed by parents anxious to bask in the glory of his material prosperity.

Negative feelings about one's Jewishness should not by any means be attributed entirely to the lack of parental concern. The Jewish teenager is involved in two cultures, two worlds of thought. To draw from both traditions simultaneously can be a doubly enriching experience, placing him in a uniquely fortunate position. However, the demands made upon him by these two worlds are occasionally competitive, each vying for his concern and attention. For example, the observant Jewish youth who attends college away from home is immediately confronted with critical decisions: Shall he modify his religious observance in a completely non-Jewish environment and make his life less complicated? Shall he eat at the fraternity house or continue to observe dietary laws at great personal inconvenience? Shall he liberalize his previously held views on sex and on going out with non-Jewish girls? Shall he ask for the special privilege of exemption from Sabbath examinations?

Furthermore, within each of these cultures the Jewish adolescent finds pluralistic and often competitive forces. In addition to being barraged by conflicting viewpoints in the school and on the street, in his home and in his neighbor's home, he is likely to meet Jewish youngsters and adults with widely varying viewpoints on Judaism. Even his religious school teachers and the rabbis with whom he has come in contact may have possibly conveyed conflicting opinions on moral and religious viewpoints. Such formidable challenges emanating from two different cultures and within the cultures themselves understandably create feelings of confusion and negation until they must be resolved by arduous reasoning which may—and does frequently—tax the resources of even the most gifted Jewish youngster.

Parents are not miracle workers. They cannot *make* their adolescents believe in or conform to a way of life that the children are unprepared to accept emotionally or intellectually. Intelligent, persuasive discussions by parents can serve the constructive purpose of helping young people understand their problems more clearly and clarify some of the conflicts produced by the clash of two cultures. But the ability to resolve these pressures, if it is to come about at all, will be achieved by the child in his own way and in his own time.

Parents should present their views forthrightly and convincingly, but if they persist in handing down pat formulas they are likely to fail.

Jewish values instilled in childhood are not lost or forgotten in the adolescent years, and parents should draw great encouragement from this as they make the conscious and often difficult effort to indoctrinate their children accordingly during the formative years. There will be periods when our young people react negatively and protestingly to this approach. But eventually, as these children find satisfaction in the adult world, there will dawn the realization that the values imparted to them in the home and school endure with brilliance and beauty.

If we adults could have a faith and a confidence in our heritage which our youngsters can rely on and to which they can continually raise their sights, then we and our children are building well for the future.

4

When Religious Differences
Arise

When a child of ten rebels in the home, it is relatively simple for parents to exert their authority, thus quashing the rebellion. For the child is still dependent upon his mother and father and is still aware of his dependency.

Not so the sixteen-year-old who now may feel that he is as mature as he will ever be. Rebellion comes easily. To challenge the established order in the home, to play the iconoclast and militate against the cherished beliefs of one's parents is not at all uncommon.

But what a blow to the parental ego! Only yesterday their opinions were eagerly sought and now this is interference and is resented.

Parents should not feel that the air of presumptuousness with which their children express themselves indicates self-confidence. They are actually less confident than ever, but are testing themselves and their newly-found knowledge. Tomorrow a new and seemingly more attractive philosophy will replace the present one, and they will show as much enthusiasm and conviction about the new as they did for the old.

If parents would realize that the critical and rebellious attitude is part of the maturing process, they will not suffer frustration or feel they have wasted their efforts. They will then meet the challenge with patience and concern, rather than with panic and disillusionment.

One of the most prevalent controversies affecting Jewish teenagers and their parents is the problem of school attendance on Jewish holidays. High school students are often reluctant to absent themselves, not merely out of fear of missing work, but because they do not wish to be considered different by the other members of the class.

Parents are often unsuccessful in their attempts to persuade their children to stay away from class. Perhaps the following approach to the problem can be attempted: In those schools where the honor system has been introduced, students have shown greater respect for its standards. There is higher regard for the teacher and less cheating on exams where one is expected to follow the dictates of his own conscience.

We Jews in America are also placed on an honor system. We are living in a voluntary Jewish society, and no one can be forced to remain absent from class on Jewish holidays. Should our conscience not lead us to attend synagogue on these days? We Jews have fought for religious freedom for centuries, and now that we have achieved it, we should not discard that for which we have fought so hard.

Furthermore, we should keep in mind those other Jewish students who want to observe the holiday. We should encourage them in their beliefs rather than give the non-Jewish teacher and student the impression that these students are just taking advantage of another opportunity to stay out of school and that they do not take their studies as seriously as we. It goes without saying that a student who decides to remain absent from class should attend synagogue on these days. To be seen attending a movie or a ball game instead of attending class is improper and hypocritical.

How do parents frequently mishandle religious problems with their recalcitrant children?

1—*They feel that someone has to take the blame.* Someone must be the culprit; either the parents, or the child, or a particular friend is responsible for the change of heart. Experience has shown that in many cases no one is really responsible for this adolescent rebellion. To insist on fixing the blame is to misunderstand the maturation process. I have myself seen teenagers coming from warm protective Jewish homes where parents attend synagogue regularly, but where those parents too are often unsuccessful in influencing their teenage children to follow their pattern. These same young people, once they have their own families, often experience for themselves the same difficulties as their parents did a generation before.

Parents would be wise to realize that despite their most earnest efforts, they may still be disappointed in their children's religious attitude. It is not at all uncommon to raise two children who will react in a completely opposite manner to the same religious stimulus in the home. All the literature on child guidance does not seem to explain adequately how the attitude and behavior of siblings can be so vastly different. Certainly the heredity factor and the realization that no two children are raised alike must be taken into account. Nevertheless, it would appear that a similar environment could harmonize at least some of the basic personality differences in children of the same family. Since we cannot completely fathom the mystery of personality, we should not feel guilty if things go wrong. We owe our children love and guidance. After that, we can only hope for the best.

Goethe deals with this theme indirectly in his *Hermann*

und Dorothea. The father rebukes his son who is about to enter into a marriage of which he violently disapproves. The wise mother speaks to her husband:

> *We have no power to fashion our*
>   *children as suits our fancy;*
> *As they are given by God, we so must*
>   *have them and love them;*
> *Teach them as best we can, and let*
>   *each of them follow his nature.*
> *One will have talents of one sort, and*
>   *different talents another.*
> *Every one uses his own, in his own*
>   *individual fashion.*

There are times, to be sure, when parents should blame themselves, particularly when they have denied their child the opportunity of obtaining a sound Jewish education. It is far better to have him challenge the validity of that which he has learned and lived with, than to be incapable of challenging altogether. In the latter case, the child has nothing to which he may return, even if later in life he so desires.

2—Likewise, *resorting to punishment or even the threat of punishment for refusal to conform is self-defeating.* There are times when parents are justified in punishing their teenage children. Disregard for the other members of the household, disrespect, and unwillingness to share in family responsibilities warrant disciplinary measures. But to impose punishment on a disbelieving child is as futile as the practice of excommunicating a heretic in our modern era. Forcing submission to belief reveals parental weakness and even cowardice or an immature refusal to face the intellectual challenge of a maturing child.

There are parents who are so disturbed with their children's noncompliance that they attempt to deprive them of gifts and allowances that were previously promised them. They seek to remind their children of their economic dependence by wielding the most punitive power that they possess. But how much is accomplished when a son or daughter who is sincerely and understandably troubled about some beliefs and practices comes to associate religion with coercion? Jacob Cohn in his book, *Modern Problems of Jewish Parents,* summarizes such an approach in these telling words: "They ask for the bread of argument and we give them the stone of power. We stand revealed in their eyes as spiritually bankrupt and not above taking unfair advantage of our position."

3—*Appealing to the child's sense of pity is also self-defeating.* When a parent exclaims that his child's non-conformity has made him ill, he is cruel to the child. In cases of mixed dating particularly, parents will work themselves into a state of hysteria, hoping that the now properly frightened child will shrink from bearing the responsibility for his parents' illness. When strength is called for, tears and emotional outbursts are acknowledgments of weakness. Better for parents to operate from a position of strength and reason, even if it means defeat, than to gain one's immediate ends while losing the admiration and respect of the child.

Parents should also keep in mind that children are usually not as interested in the reaction of neighbors and relatives as they are, and to appeal to a child's sense of shame and embarrassment for strange behavior may prove quite ineffective. Most adolescents are not affected by neighborhood gossip, especially if they feel that their own friends are on their side.

4—Finally, *parents dare not seek to control the child's sources of information, even when they are convinced that they are absorbing misinformation.* If our teenagers are intellectually alert, they should feel free to read those books that satisfy this curiosity, and if parents seek to limit them, forbidden books will be that much more tempting and enticing. Today's instructor who may engage the immediate attention of young people will, in all likelihood, be superseded by others in the course of time who will help to balance the philosophical and religious outlook of the youngster. Just as it is inadvisable to shelter the child from all groups of people for fear of the unwholesome influence of some, so is it unrealistic to expect an inquisitive student to avoid contact with the writings of a Bertrand Russell, a Robert Ingersoll or a Karl Marx. T. V. Smith put it succinctly when he wrote: "To tell a man what to think is in every long run the working equivalent of telling him not to think at all."

Of course, interested parents can help their youngsters develop their reading along sound religious lines by having appropriate books readily available in the home library or by more formal, well-planned guidance of the child's reading.

This discussion on reading is unfortunately irrelevant in many families. In all too many homes teenagers read just enough to get by in school and consequently rarely seek out great books on their own initiative. Their parents confine their own reading to the daily newspapers, current best sellers, or very practical technical books relating to their particular vocations.[1]

When parents begin to understand that they can despite

---

[1] Gordon Dupee reports that 25 per cent of the college graduates say they have not read one book in a year; only 17 per cent of adults, at any time, are reading a book; only 12 per cent of the houses being constructed will have built-in bookcases, and 42 per cent of American homes have no bookcases at all; only 13 per cent of Americans borrow books from the public libraries; and, librarians estimate only 5 per cent of these are good reading, 7 per cent are of fair quality, and 88 per cent are of low quality. Mr. Dupee says, "We are asking the next generation to exhibit a virtue of mind which we ourselves have debased through indifference and disuse." "Can Johnny's Parents Read?"—*Saturday Review,* June 2, 1956.

the best intentions mishandle situations involving their child's anti-religious attitudes, they will also better understand the positive approaches that can be taken as a remedy.

A—*Our reactions should be natural.* Even though we may be surprised to hear our once agreeable child minimize belief in God or tradition, we would do well to let him know that we went through a stage of disbelief ourselves and that we were not sheltered in the least from conflicting theories in our youth. The same knowing I'm-not-so-naive attitude should be displayed when the child comes home with newly discovered theories on love and sex. Mother and father should find some satisfaction in knowing that their child is willing to open up lines of communication on the subject. Too many youngsters fear their parents' reaction, or they just don't feel that their parents are interested in their views. But when they themselves bring up such problems, they are inviting debate, which can have constructive results provided that we do not appear disarmed, shocked or personally offended.

B—*Respect his individuality.* A child who never deviates from convention is admittedly easier to live with than the rugged individualist, but the latter compensates in many ways for the problems he creates. He challenges, he stimulates, he adds luster to family living.

The parent, in explaining his opposing views to the youngster, might preface his remarks with a note of encouragement: "I respect you for your views even though I can't agree with them," or "I'm happy that you are really thinking about the problem. I would not want you to accept blindly what I have told you."

We do not speak now of the adolescent who offensively dismisses any view that the parent may wish to offer. Filial disrespect needs the firmer and less congratulatory response so adequately prescribed in the Passover Haggaddah, namely, to answer the impetuous son in the spirit of his question.

C—*Maintain your integrity.* Even if parents cannot convince their child of the soundness of their beliefs, they should unhesitatingly retain their principles. As important as harmony is to the household, it is far more desirable for parents to suffer the risks of disunity rather than relinquish their cherished beliefs to make things easier for the youngster.

Time and again, religious leaders hear parents say that they gave up maintaining a kosher home because their children insisted that certain foods be brought into the house. I am acquainted with a family whose parents gave up synagogue membership because the children made them believe that the membership dues were not being used for a more practical purpose. Parents must insist on their own individuality just as they respect that of their child. They gain neither love nor respect by compromising with their ideals. They cannot, nor should they want to, force their beliefs on their children, and they should understand they must be on the alert too, for children can and do sometimes take unfair advantage of their flexibility. Children should always be in a position to move into a stronger position of belief and practice if they later desire to do so. They should feel that the door is always open to them and that their parents will always welcome their return to accepted religious practices.

D—*Show consistency in thought and action.* The pressures of everyday living make consistency difficult. Many ordinarily high-minded people find themselves compromising their ideals in their business and professional activity. They will often choose the path of expediency even when aware that it is against their better judgment.

A youngster who has expressed negative feelings about his

parents' religious beliefs will now be constantly on the look-out for self-justification. He will quickly exploit those inconsistencies between theory and practice, if not openly, at least to himself in order to fortify his skeptical position. Disrespect between parents, quarrelsomeness, untruthfulness, gossip in the household will hinder the child's chances for reconciliation with religious faith at a later stage in his development.

Norman Podhoretz, in an article entitled *Where Is The Beat Generation Going?* observes, "The combination of hypocrisy with a paralysis of parental authority is beautifully contrived to turn the children loose to make their own rules, and the rules they make are invariably the rules of the street."

During adolescence, elders are looked upon more realistically by the child than in the younger years. The teenager is by now aware of his parents' imperfections. These he can learn to respect as something natural to all human beings. But he does expect fair mindedness, tolerance, and integrity from his parents even though he may not quite live up to these qualifications himself; and the impressions that he will carry with him of his parents may determine very largely his attitude toward his God in future years. Atheism is often the result of shifting a grudge onto God because of one's disappointment with his father or mother. Conversely, it is natural to attribute those positive qualities to God which one has seen in his parents during his youth.

Everything that has been written in this chapter is predicated on the assumption that the parents themselves react positively to religion in general and to Jewish tradition in particular. Some youngsters find they must defend Jewish tradition in the presence of apathetic parents who in their youth had little Jewish education or who rebelled against their childhood training without ever having sought a reconciliation. These "inverted rebels" experience more than the discomfort of loneliness; they are occasionally ridiculed and berated for disrupting the family harmony with their demands. Sigmund Freud, though himself a non-observing Jew, nevertheless recognized the importance of parental encouragement. Writing to Max Graf, he observed: "If you do not let your son grow up as a Jew, you deprive him of those sources of energy which cannot be replaced by anything else. He will have to struggle as a Jew and you ought to develop in him all the energy he will need for the struggle. Do not deprive him of that advantage."

Above all else, parents of teenagers should distinguish between the effort to guide and to control their children's lives. Our young people need wise but firm parental guidance in developing wholesome religious, cultural and social attitudes. They will profit immeasurably from intelligence and experience when it is offered with unselfish interest. But many parents attempt to control, and despite their insistence that they are trying to help their children, they are rather fulfilling a selfish psychological need in themselves. In effect, they are showing resentment toward their children who are growing rapidly into vigorous adults, with all their successes ahead of them, while they, the parents, must confront the reality that they have already passed their prime and are now declining in vigor and strength. The failure to come to grips with this motivation constitutes one of the real obstacles that impedes a sound parent-child relationship. Many parents simply work too hard at developing their children when they are in reality interfering with development by prolonging adolescence in order to keep their children submissive and dependent.

The great German rabbi, Samson Raphael Hirsch, likened the Eternal Light in the sanctuary to the student in the classroom. Just as the priest applied the flame until the flame ascended of its own, so the task of the teacher is to make the student independent of him. In the same manner, the task of the parent consists largely of developing a sense of independence and self-reliance in the child. The measure of success of a marriage or a family, of a nation or a society, is the extent to which it makes possible the maximum development of the potentialities of the individuals within it. And we parents can impart this to our teenagers, not so much by what we say to them as by treating them as individuals worthy of our respect. The adolescent needs to feel that his parents respect him primarily as a person and do not regard him merely as a child to be loved.

5

Jewish Ethics for the Teenager

Jewish adolescents are prone to identify religion merely with ritual and not with ethics even though they are aware that Judaism contains ethical principles. Bernard Rosen, whose study of adolescents has already been cited, asked his three groups of teenagers to estimate how religious they were and to explain how they arrived at this self-estimate. Since Judaism is a system of beliefs, ethical concepts, and practices, one would expect that the teenager's opinion would be formed within the framework of these three components. Rosen found, however, that for the overwhelming majority, religion was associated primarily with the extent of ritual observance. Adolescents who describe themselves as "strongly" or "moderately" religious were usually those who observed the dietary laws and attended synagogue regularly. The adolescents who called themselves "slightly" or "not at all" religious were the least observant. Furthermore, Rosen's study indicated that adolescents frequently cited persons known to them whose ethics were questionable but whom they nevertheless considered religious because of their observance of Jewish ritual.

This separate identification of religion and ethics is frequently retained throughout adulthood and constitutes one of the most serious obstacles to a proper understanding of the nature of Judaism.

Judaism and ethics are inseparable. The ancient Jews never thought of ethics as a special science, or as a branch of philosophy, as did the Greeks. God was conceived of as a moral God who demanded ethical behavior of His children. Just as God is holy, so should man created in His image aspire to holiness. Our textbook of morality is the Bible. In it we discover God's will, His moral requirements as revealed to the priests, judges, and prophets who, in turn, interpreted these requirements to the people. The influence of Jewish ethics on our western civilization has been so far-reaching that it is virtually impossible to fully appraise its extent, to know where Jewish ethics leaves off and non-Jewish ethics begins. For centuries, philosophers, statesmen, artists and poets have drawn their creative inspiration directly from the Bible or at least indirectly from sources that were originally inspired by Biblical sources.

Shakespeare was well acquainted with Biblical thought and style, using Biblical terms and allusions with ease. Tennyson was saturated with Biblical content. Our own James Russell Lowell, Henry W. Longfellow, and John G. Whittier were all greatly influenced by the Bible. Matthew Arnold made the Bible his constant companion. Nicholas Murray Butler said on one occasion: "Without the Bible, it is impossible to understand the literature of the English language from Chaucer to Browning." Solomon Goldman devotes six hundred pages of his *Echoes and Allusions* to the Book of Genesis alone, drawn from European and American authors. And even this collection is only a sampling of all the references to a single book of the Bible.

The Biblical spirit pervades our great national documents,

such as the Declaration of Independence and the Constitution of the United States. The Bible is an indispensable source book for the understanding of our entire American heritage.

And yet what is startling is the apparent lack of moral sensitivity in a society that has been so aware of these concepts and principles. Morality at first glance would seem to be uppermost in our minds; no people moralize as much as we do. Our schools, houses of worship, our fraternal and civic organizations are founded on the highest moral principles. Yet it appears that lawlessness and immorality are almost as prevalent here as in those societies where people need only abide by the most primitive codes. We read and hear of prominent civic leaders and children of renowned parents who violate the most basic legal and moral standards for reasons often unknown to students of human and social behavior.

Undoubtedly there is much to be said for the many theories that have been propounded by sociologists and psychiatrists to explain these apparently strange patterns of behavior. Surely, economic problems can be held partially responsible for moral breakdown, but where do the sons and daughters of wealthy parents fit into this thesis? The attempt to explain immorality or delinquency in terms of parental rejection or the absence of love sometimes has great merit, but even emotional security has not always prevented indecency.

My own feeling is that we have overlooked a simple factor, far less complicated than those proposed by our students of science. Our people have been inculcated with the theoretical principles of religion, but they have not sufficiently applied these theories in their daily lives. They may quote Biblical passages or lofty pronouncements from historic documents, but they fail in the task of making them relevant in daily living and for their own particular problems. They know the Biblical dictum, "Thou shalt love thy neighbor as thyself," and they will attest that they firmly believe in it,

but they will fail to use it practically when confronted with
the specific problems pertaining to their relationship with
others. They will agree in theory that the Fatherhood of God
and the Brotherhood of Man represent the noblest concepts,
but they refuse to believe that they must renounce their
cherished belief in racial or religious segregation.

Vance Packard devotes a whole chapter in his book, *The
Status Seekers,* to the clannishness of America's churches,
pointing out that the more prosperous Protestant denomina-
tions are so class-conscious that they discourage the less successful to affiliate with them or to worship with them. As for
Negroes, we all know of their uphill struggle to merely worship in so-called white churches. He concludes with the wry
comment that "at present, the brotherhood of man is in danger of becoming a nice intellectual concept."

It has been the Jewish belief that the Torah speaks to all
people regardless of age, background, or mental capacity.
Parents and educators should endeavor to interpret Biblical
concepts for their children by applying Jewish ethics to situations in which adolescents are daily involved. Unless the teenager can feel that the Torah speaks to him as a child of the
twentieth century living in the city or in the suburbs or on
the farm, then the study of Bible is an anachronistic as the
study of alchemy or astrology.

Before parents can begin to make ethics relevant to their
teenage children they should establish the proper framework
for ethical living by attempting to clarify the basic reasons
for what is accepted as correct ethical and moral behavior.

If faith in God means anything, it should be more than
just believing in His existence. It should mean that God requires of us the standards of morality set forth in the Bible. If
we genuinely believe in Him, then we are prepared to search
out His requirements and live up to them even though there

may be no prizes or material rewards for following them. More important, we learn that there are often greater material rewards in ignoring moral laws. Honesty is not always the best policy, if "best" is taken to mean the most rewarding materially. Dishonest people don't always get caught. But people of genuine faith are willing to take great chances because they feel that conviction is the most precious virtue a man can possess. We become so confident in the truth of God's law that we are willing to defend it and fight for it and will never surrender it for convenience.

The rabbinic tradition stresses that goodness is its own reward. The reward of performing an act of goodness is simply that it results in our doing other acts of goodness. Our nature then becomes so accustomed to goodness that we are repelled by evil in ourselves and in others.

This does not mean that God expects perfection from us. God knows our faults better than we ourselves. We should not feel that just because we cannot be perfect we can therefore not be good. We are termed "good" when we recognize our faults and work toward self-improvement by keeping the Torah-goals constantly before us.

What are some of these Torah-goals which we speak of and how may they be applied by the parents of teenagers? Let us take a few verses from Leviticus, Chapter 19, in which the essentials of the whole Torah are summarized. Here are some problems which the teenagers themselves or their parents have brought to me during the past two years:

A—*Problem:* "How can someone with my busy schedule in and out of school be expected to stop and think about God all the time? People in the past were not nearly as busy as the average youngster today. Their interests were not as varied. Their education was primarily religious, giving them much more time to pray and to concentrate on their faith."

Verse 2—"Ye shall be holy, for I, the Lord your God, am holy."

Interpretation—Religion includes prayer and contemplation, but primarily it concerns itself with righteousness. Prayer and Torah study are important mainly because they lead to holiness, and human holiness does not imply anything more than an attempt to imitate the goodness of God in the best way we know. God represents the ultimate in truth, loving kindness, justice, and honesty. Whenever we perform an act of truth, loving kindness, justice or honesty, we fulfill the prescription of holiness because we have imitated God's way. Now who will deny that every person, young or old, has many opportunities during the course of a busy day to perform these acts of goodness, while at the same time remembering that these acts are also links between God and man, and that man is nearest to God at these times!

B—*Problem:* "My mother and father are young and modern people. They like to go out on Saturday evenings and they enjoy many of the same forms of entertainment that I do. In fact, the whole family is sort of young at heart, and yet there are times when they just put up a big wall between them and myself. They check on the time I get home in the evening. They still insist that I ask to be excused before leaving the table. Sometimes I feel that they are far stricter than my teachers."

Verse 3—"Ye shall stand in awe every man of his mother and father. . . ."

Interpretation—The Torah here emphasizes the importance of reverence or respect for parents. Parents are of course expected to be warm and sympathetic toward their children, and there are times when they should relax and be informal with their sons and daughters. But children should never come to look upon their parents as they would their school chums; they should always look to their parents with respect and reverence. Parents *are* in many ways like teachers, perhaps even more so, for they are the teachers of a lifetime.

Samuel Belkin in his *Essays on Traditional Jewish Thought* writes: "The art of teaching does not consist only of instruction in the three R's. There is more to teaching than conveying technical information. Teaching is the continuous process of building character, establishing moral attitudes, creating respect for the good way of life and distaste for the lightheaded and irresponsible mode of existence."

Experience has indicated that even those children who may have formerly resented the association of parents as teachers and disciplinarians almost invariably looked back in gratitude to parents who insisted on standards, provided those standards were reasonable. There is no substitute for the feeling of security that comes with parents who can give appropriate direction to their children.

C—*Problem:* "I was penalized in high school last week for having shared my test answers with the boy across the table. The irony of it all was that we both got the wrong answers. I just don't think I really did anything wrong since I was helping a friend in need."

Verse 14—"Thou shalt not curse the deaf nor put a stumbling block before the blind, but thou shalt revere God; I am the Lord."

Interpretation—Naturally, we like to help others in need, but there are times when despite good intentions we hinder others rather than help them. This cannot be considered a criminal act, but it is a subtle wrong, the consequences of which could lead to more serious wrongs. It makes little difference whether we offer the correct or the incorrect answer. By such an act we encourage our friend to rely on others when he is expected to rely on himself. He was not wise in asking for the answer, and you were neither generous nor farsighted in offering it. Your friend must not feel that he can get through school merely by relying on the efforts of others.

It goes without saying that we are putting the "stumbling block before the blind" when we deliberately give wrong advice to another, thus helping him to commit an unnecessary wrong. And we incite an ordinarily harmless person to resort to brute force by deliberately angering him when we violate this Biblical command.

The first part of this verse, "To curse the deaf," if understood in its broad sense, would include the prohibition of blackballing a pledgee for membership in a fraternity by accusing him of wrongdoing without giving him an opportunity to face his accuser and to defend himself. This was unfortunately a common practice in some investigating committees of the United States Senate until some highly ethical congressmen, urged on by outraged public opinion, recognized the injustice of this practice and insisted that the accused be permitted to be present when accusations were made against him.

D—*Problem:* "I really made an enemy yesterday. Gail became violently angry with me because I told the girls what really happened to her father. He was fined by the government for income tax evasion. After all, I wasn't slandering anyone, since what I said was true, wasn't it?"

Verse 16—"Thou shalt not go up and down as a talebearer amongst thy people. . . ."

Interpretation—The Torah is not only concerned with

slander but also with malicious gossip which may be true, but is nevertheless a violation of ethics. Since the law penalizes a man for his violations, surely we should not punish him further by causing others to be bitter against him. To completely destroy a person's reputation is to take away his most precious possession, and even though he may be foolish enough to ruin his own reputation by breaking the law, we should attempt to help him become rehabilitated. It has been wisely said that gossip kills three—the person who is spreading it, the person who is listening to it and the person about whom the gossip is spread. The Book of Proverbs puts it simply but penetratingly when it says, "Where no wood is, the fire will go out, and where there is no whisperer, the contention ceases."

The second part of this verse reads, "Neither shall thou stand idly by the blood of thy neighbor; I am the Lord." In a sense, this verse may be understood as having a direct relation to the previous part of the verse. If a person is being slandered and we have evidence to the contrary, it is our responsibility to refute the slanderer. We cannot keep silent at such a crucial time, and even if the rumor be true, we should protect the accused from the accuser by showing sympathy and understanding for his unfortunate predicament. To remain silent when another is attacked in our presence is sometimes more prudent than agreeing with the accuser, but it is better and nobler to defend the accused, thus opening the eyes of the accuser.

E—*Problem:* "My friend could easily have been voted the most popular boy in the class, but he has the peculiar habit of criticizing the other fellow. I won't say that his criticism is wrong. I'll admit he is usually right, but he still creates a lot of resentment.

Verse 17—". . . .Thou shalt surely rebuke they neighbor and not bear sin because of him."

Interpretation—This friend must have a great deal of character if he is willing to sacrifice popularity in order to help a friend see his self-destructive faults. Few people appreciate criticism even when it is constructive. Most of us prefer flattery to fact, but we must recognize there are genuinely high-minded people who feel a deep sense of responsibility for their fellow man and are impelled to point out their faults to them. If they fail to remind others of these faults, then they feel they are "bearing sin because of him." Naturally, our criticism should be gentle and it should be constructive. It should be given in private so that there is no embarrassment, for otherwise our best intentions will be deeply resented. It must also be emphasized that a critic should be certain that he does not possess the very faults he sees in others. ("Do not rebuke your neighbor for a blemish which you possess.") We are also reminded by the sages to put ourselves in the position of the other man to determine how we would act were we in similar circumstances.

F—*Problem:* "We have had a German exchange student in our school for the past seven months and, knowing what the Germans did to my mother's family, I just can't bring myself to befriend him. Every time I pass him in the hall I curse him underneath my breath and secretly wish that he would taste some of the tragedy that my mother's family suffered in his homeland."

Verse 18—"Thou shalt not take vengeance nor bear any grudge against the children of thy people. . . ."

Interpretation—It is so natural for people to bear grudges and to seek revenge that only extraordinary people can discipline themselves by rising above their instincts. The Torah does not prescribe the path that is easiest to follow but requires us to choose the path that will bring us closer to God's character. And just as He is forgiving, so must we strive to be forgiving.

We are not asked to forget what happened to the Jewish people at the hands of the Germans under Hitler. Our people and, indeed, all humanity, must remember that incredible tragedy and outrage so that we may be more alert to such misfortunes in the future. But at the same time we have a moral responsibility toward those Germans and others who were not yet born or who were too young to have protested against German barbarism, for in so doing we show them that we still have faith in the new generation and that the innocent need not suffer from the crimes of their parents or their countrymen.

Every teenage ethical problem is not covered in the Bible, just as the Bible cannot yield answers to all our contemporary problems. Nevertheless, the Bible's store of moral wisdom is all but limitless and we can and should return to it throughout life.

It is often difficult for parents to apply Biblical insights to their child's ethical problems, but there are excellent Bible aids, such as the Hertz and Soncino commentaries on the Pentateuch, which help to clarify many sections.

Two additional important objectives are achieved by utilizing the Bible for the discussion of ethical problems: (1) The parent helps to re-establish the integrity and prestige of the Bible to a generation of Jews that knows little of its contents or influence; and (2) if a parent has any doubt about the practicability of his own advice in helping solve a moral problem, the Bible offers a type of wisdom which has endured for centuries.

To most people the Bible represents the word of God at least in the form of divine inspiration; to others it is superb literature which has no equal. Only a few have denied its value as a classic handbook of ethical living.

A reminder to parents: In exploring the Bible for the purpose of finding a solution to our moral dilemmas, let us not merely seek support for our preconceived notions, for we can, if we are willing to distort the Bible by quoting out of context, find support for the most destructive philosophies. If one wishes to look at isolated passages without concerning himself with the Book as an interrelated unit, he may find support for such extreme points of view as forced conversion, war-mongering, or racial discrimination. The Bible, like a drug, can have a lethal effect on those who do not deal with it effectively. That is why it becomes imperative to seek the aid of good translations and commentaries. Otherwise we shall find ourselves in waters too deep and too turbulent for the average reader. The rabbi in your community, by virtue of his years of specialized training, is in most cases eminently qualified to present a course on ethics for adults. If your congregation does not offer such a course, it could probably be arranged through the efforts of a group of parents who request it. Even when formal classes are not feasible, specific questions concerning Biblical interpretations are usually greeted by the rabbi as a welcome challenge.

Prof. Louis Finklestein, commenting on the place of ethics in the life of the businessman, writes:

"The businessman can without 'moralizing' (which would be deadening and self-defeating) transform his home into a school for moral responsibility. Avoiding precept, the businessman can make even his conversation at table serve the vital end of character education for himself, his wife, his children, and his guests. The stories he tells, the gestures he makes, the conversation he chooses and avoids, can all show that he has at least some notion of what life, America, and freedom are about. Without being in the slightest degree priggish, and eventually without self-consciousness, he may help his family and friends obtain insight into the ethical life."

It is axiomatic that family discussions on the importance of ethical living have no value unless parents are scrupulously moral in their daily living. Though teaching by precept has its definite place, teaching by example is a far more effective instrument. Parents should be prepared to search diligently for inconsistencies in their own ethical beliefs and practices when they feel their children have become transgressors. A parent disappointed in a child who cheats in a school examination does not encourage honesty when he pads an expense account or shades the truth in an income tax return. Even the man who manages to remain within bounds of the law, but who is constantly seeking loopholes for his own advantage, vitiates the moral atmosphere in the home.

Nahmanides, a thirteenth-century Spanish sage, commenting on the verse "ye shall be holy; for I the Lord your God am holy," observed that there is a vast difference between the legal and the holy in life. A man, he says, can observe the letter of the law and still be a rogue. Such a man may never have been called into court, and yet he is as unscrupulous as those who break the law. The purpose of our religion is to sanctify, to teach one to do not only what the law requires, but what is proper in the eyes of God.

The teenager's struggle for the family car receives considerable attention in the press almost daily. Unable to wait until he has his own car, the youngster takes the keys without permission and stealthily goes out in the family car for a ride with friends. Now, this is more than a breach of ethics, but a threat to the safety of other drivers. The parents are usually quick to reprimand the youngster by restricting his most desirable privileges. And yet, does not this all-too-common youthful behavior reflect a misdirected emphasis in upbringing by the parent? The child has been made to feel that material possessions are symbols of prestige and power, and the more numerous and glittering those possessions, the greater the prestige of the individual. There is nothing reprehensible about a youngster driving the family car, or owning a relatively inexpensive car, for that matter; but when he regards the automobile as the fulfillment of his greatest objective, it is symptomatic of misplaced emphasis by the parents.

It is noteworthy that today not only underprivileged youngsters have been apprehended for stealing, but also children of well-to-do families who candidly admit that their parents provided them with handsome allowances. The parents must bear some of this responsibility, not only for having failed to instill respect for the property of others, but also for having given their children the impression that there should be no limit to their desire for material possessions. These youngsters become convinced that the more they have the more fortunate they are; and as soon as they have obtained their immediate material goals, they must set up new objectives with new possessions. The historian Lecky once remarked that to expand one's circle of wants is to multiply temptation and thus increase the number of sins. And long before Lecky, the great sage Ben Zoma defined a wealthy man as one who was content with his portion. These are the great lessons for our teenagers.

Russell Lynes, managing editor of *Harper's Magazine*, reminds all adults that the teenager is also a mirror of many—perhaps too many—of our own characteristics. "It is easy to take this sub-culture group, the teenagers," he says, "and read our characters and future in them as though they were tea leaves. We can see adumbrated in them our attitudes toward religion, toward the arts and toward education more clearly than we can by looking at ourselves. We are likely to be more indulgent in looking at ourselves than at them; we smooth over our own exaggerations while we view theirs with alarm."

6

Bar and Bat Mitzvah——
The Threshold of Adolescence

If the Bar Mitzvah ceremony indicated vitality in the American Jewish community, there would be no need to wonder about the revival of Judaism in America. No ceremony, with the exception of circumcision and marriage, is observed so widely by American Jewry.

We must admit that the Bar Mitzvah has proven itself to be a mixed blessing. Much can still be said in its favor. In anticipation of the event, enrollment in a religious school is usually accepted without question. Many more children are receiving religious education today than they did twenty-five years ago, and enrollment figures confirm this beyond question. In the suburbs, particularly among the younger married couples and growing families, the growth of religious school enrollment is phenomenal. The mere fact that children are in the school until the age of thirteen, notwithstanding the obvious motives of some parents, presents an exciting challenge to the best type of Jewish educator. Given a sound school system and a group of devoted and able teachers, the intellectual and emotional needs of the child during these receptive years can be developed to a high degree. And many parents too have during such a period been known to develop a taste for Jewish tradition or to reaffirm their dormant Jewish loyalties. For the child's period of study in the Hebrew school summons up in his elders at home old memories and deep feelings for the genuine values of their heritage which may have been submerged for many years.

The Bar Mitzvah ceremony is experienced at a most opportune stage in the child's development, at the threshold of adolescence itself. Just at the time when a child craves reassurance of his parents' love and an added measure of self-confidence, he becomes the center of his home life. His parents thus help to bolster his lagging sense of self-esteem by their obvious pride in his achieving distinction—even if only for a day—for the whole family. Relatives and friends come from distant cities to participate in this *simcha* for which he has prepared so meticulously for many months.

There are, however, disquieting aspects to the great event which the less sensitive should be fully aware of. All this anticipation leading up to a momentous event is often a prelude to the great letdown that follows. The child has been lifted to such emotional heights that he is most anxious to be relieved of all the discipline and responsibility that comes afterward. He knows that after Bar Mitzvah he need not pursue advanced study and that his parents usually do not care, and as a result he will quite often abruptly drop his recently awakened interest in Jewish life and culture.

Unless the child is unusually inquisitive or religiously inclined, there is probably little encouragement to continue one's studies. Most of his friends have managed to withdraw quietly from Hebrew School after their Bar Mitzvah without disrupting family harmony. These friends seem to have found a new unfettered freedom, and they are frequently successful in persuading the newly-confirmed youngster to emulate them.[1]

Parents will not deliberately prevent the child from continuing his Jewish education, but they often fail to impress upon the child the importance of remaining in Hebrew School. Parents tend to be overly sympathetic with the son's complaint about the allegedly demanding schedule he has had to keep since enrolling in the religious school.

But far more disrupting than this is the impression of the Bar Mitzvah that is often left with the child. In spite of the efforts of his teachers to emphasize the sacredness of the Bar Mitzvah Sabbath, most of the planning and excitement in the home is centered around the Bar Mitzvah incidentals—the reception, the entertainment, the invitation list, the clothing.[2]

[1] A recent survey of Jewish education in this country published by the American Association for Jewish Education reveals that while the number of children receiving instruction has increased appreciably in recent years, the problem of continuing after Bar and Bas Mitzvah still remains unsolved. 71 per cent of the Jewish school population is concentrated in the first three grades and only 2.5 per cent is enrolled in the high school department.

[2] *The New York Post* recently reported an incident which, though unusual in itself, represents a common misconception regarding the importance of the Bar Mitzvah reception.

The parents of a Bar Mitzvah candidate who were in moderate circumstances had contracted with a caterer for a reception for eighty persons at a cost of $695.95. The boy had a trust fund of $606.40 awarded him in a personal injury suit, and the parents asked permission to use all of it to pay the caterer.

In his decision the judge said: "The Bar Mitzvah ceremony is a solemnization of a boy's becoming a 'son of the Commandment' and should encourage him in the paths of righteousness. It was never intended to be a vehicle for mere entertainment and display.

"The spiritual values the occasion symbolizes may not be relegated to second place in favor of a gesture of conspicuous consumption. It would be more fitting if the funds belonging to this boy were utilized to initiate, or to continue, his education in faith and morals.

"While it is manifest that it was never intended that the principal feature of the Bar Mitzvah festivities be an epicurean adventure, the solemnity of the occasion need not render it less joyous, for the Psalmist has enjoined us to 'serve the Lord in gladness.'

In this spirit the court grants the application to the extent of permitting the withdrawal of $200."

The non-kosher reception held out of the Synagogue on Saturday afternoon with music and entertainment, smoking and pic-
ture-taking, does not merely confuse the child but reduces the
entire religious ceremony to insignificance. More and more
one hears of relatives and friends who fail to attend the service,
but enthusiastically appear at the gala reception on Saturday
evening or Sunday afternoon. Some parents have expressed
disappointment at the poor turnout of relatives on Shabbat
morning, but their egos are reinflated by the time the reception has ended. By then they have received compliments on
the ingenious choice of a miraculous caterer and incompara-
ble orchestra; and then to cap this off, it turns out that the
cash and other gifts to the lad have surpassed their expectations. They are delighted that the months of planning have
brought such rich rewards, tangible and intangible. For some
days and weeks they will fondly recall their great week end,
but it will be the memory of a social event only. For somehow
the profound significance of the Bar Mitzvah ceremony often
seems to get lost in the excitement of what is essentially a religious celebration.[3]

This is not meant to be a satire on the emptiness of American Judaism. It is an attempt to point up the startling fact
that the Bar Mitzvah with all of its present-day social emphasis
has become so secularized that the purpose for which it was
intended has become lost to both parent and child. And unless we can begin again to simplify the Bar Mitzvah, to give
it the classic solemnity as well as joyousness of fifty or one
hundred years ago, the entire institution will become little

---

[3] Rabbi Ira Eisenstein wrote in his congregational bulletin about some of
these abuses of the Bar Mitzvah, and issued the following warning: "In
school we try to inculcate the power to discriminate between what is trivial,
between the good and the merely glittering. Then comes the Bar Mitzvah
party which so often neutralizes all that the school has attempted to teach,
and influences the child to believe that ostentation is better than modesty,
and that money spent on elaborate entertainment is better spent than money
spent on books, charity or the synagogue."

more than a grand social event not unlike the presentation of young debutantes to society.

The Bar Mitzvah should be looked upon as a natural transitional stage from childhood to adolescence in which the boy is now accorded full status in the synagogue, but in which his Jewish education is not interrupted or disturbed. It should be deemed an honor which is to be earned by the child rather than a celebration accorded him merely because he has reached the age of thirteen.

It has been well established by now that teenagers want a realistic set of moral standards, some guiding principles to help them work through the inconsistencies and problems of everyday living. They seek two basic objectives: (1) A sense of security that a society such as ours does not give them; and (2) a feeling of emotional satisfaction that the scientific world around them has not provided. Modern science explains a great deal to these children but hardly touches the problem of purpose and destiny in life. The desire to change the world and to do some good for humanity is very strong during adolescence, partly because such ideals fire the adolescent imagination and partly because adolescent hopes have not yet been sullied by disappointment and cynicism.

Parents may play a vital role in fulfilling emotional needs of their children, but only if they as parents and adults have a world view of their own. Unfortunately, children are often confused by the lack of a consistent philosophy among their elders. That is why they so often turn to their contemporaries for guidance and away from their elders. The Hebrew high school therefore, besides teaching language skills, should, and often does, help to provide direction in developing a world outlook and a philosophy of living.

Parents can begin to prepare their children long in advance of their Haftarah preparation in the Hebrew School by indoctrinating them with a true understanding of the significance of the Bar Mitzvah and the necessity for continuing their Jewish education beyond Bar Mitzvah. Here are some approaches:

A—Up until Bar Mitzvah you have been a Jew by accident of birth. You haven't had the opportunity of *choosing* the religion that you are to follow, since being born of Jewish parents automatically makes you a Jew. After Bar Mitzvah you proclaim in effect that you remain a Jew by choice. Now that you have begun to understand the meaning of the Jewish way of life, your status will no longer be that of a draftee but a volunteer. Before God and the Jewish people you will attest that you are a Jew by choice and you will place upon your own shoulders the responsibility of living as a Jew.

B—Every positive Jew, and we hope you choose to be one, should look upon himself as holding a twofold citizenship. Politically, you are a citizen of the country in which you live; but you are also a "spiritual citizen" of world Jewry. Just as every political citizen is called upon to abide by certain basic principles of the Constitution and to protect his country when its existence is threatened, so every "citizen" of world Jewry should uphold the essential principles of the Torah, which is, in a sense, the Jewish Constitution, and to help defend its people and its spiritual homeland, Israel, from attack. Our Jewish civilization can be destroyed, either by enemies from without, such as the Pharaohs, the Hamans, and the Hitlers, or by the enemies from within, by those victims of self-hatred who look upon their Jewish birth as a tragedy. The future survival of Judaism will require courage, alertness, and firm determination on the part of all affirmative Jews.

C—The most important way for "Citizens of World Jewry" to equip themselves in this struggle for survival is through

Jewish education. The Jewish education you are receiving before Bar Mitzvah is naturally limited because the mind is not prepared to grasp the really great ideas and concepts of Judaism until after the age of thirteen. With further study we shall be able to understand more and more of the vast but harmonious pattern of our religious heritage. The ideas *behind* the stories in the Bible, the *meaning* of Jewish history, the richness and vitality of the Hebrew language all are part of the immense and stirring Jewish heritage.

D—Jewish education is not less important than your public school education. One prepares primarily for your American citizenship and the other for your "Citizenship in World Jewry." It is true that our Jewish education, unlike our public school studies, is not intended to prepare us for a career unless we expect to enter the field of Jewish service. But, on the other hand, our public school education does not give us insights into many of our spiritual and moral problems: Why was I born? What is my purpose on this earth? What is my relationship to the universe? Why do men suffer? Our public schools are not concerned with learning how to accept one's Jewishness with satisfaction and joy. Man needs answers to these questions too. In many ways these questions are at least as vital and practical to us as the mysteries of algebra and science in junior high school.

E—Each of the fifty states determines the minimum age for compulsory school attendance. Although no state requires the completion of high school, most young people are prudent enough to want to finish high school. An increasing number are attending college. No one can force a Jewish child to continue his Jewish education after the age of thirteen, or, for that matter, to begin it. But we injure ourselves by not continuing our Jewish education just as surely as we do when we do not continue our secular studies into high school and beyond.

F—It is a simple matter to follow those friends who choose to discontinue their Jewish studies after the age of thirteen. No effort is required for such behavior. But to be an individual, to assert one's own character, requires a strong will and moral courage. One gains much more satisfaction in knowing that others will follow our choice than to blindly follow those who choose the easy path. What would have happened to the growth of our country in the nineteenth century without those pioneers who always reached out for new frontiers? Without such men and women to lead, a society decays. If our young people can help make Jewish learning fashionable after Bar Mitzvah by setting the pace, by their example, they shall take their place alongside a great and distinguished group of Jewish pioneers of the past who have contributed to the ever-recurring vitality of Jewish life.

G—There is also the practical problem of retaining information that may be profitably pointed out to the child. William Chomsky, a prominent Jewish educator, reminds us that the mind is a poor storage tank. "It is full of leaks through which factual material learned, and not used, has a discouraging tendency to evaporate and disappear." This observation has been borne out by psychological studies showing that, on the average, fifty per cent of what we learned is forgotten within six months to a year. After a two-year period we many expect to forget as much as eighty per cent of that which we have learned.

What has been said of the boy's education is equally applicable to the advanced education of the girl. Parents who regard the education of the boy as far more important fail to understand the vital role of the mother in Jewish life. Judaism is basically home-centered, and the girl's education is in many ways more vital than that of the boy, for she in turn will become the mother who spends more time in the home with the child. There seems to be no valid reason, excepting perhaps the religious objection of the Orthodox, to deny the girl the same privileges and responsibilities accorded the boy. Speaking of Bar Mitzvah, Abraham Segal, the prominent Jewish educator, writes: "Intelligent informed women are just as vital to community welfare in Jewish religious life as intelligent informed men. A girl should certainly be welcomed into our community as warmly as a boy."

In addition to the positive reasons that may be given for Bar Mitzvah, it must be noted that in many families where there are both sons and daughters, deep feelings of hostility and envy have been expressed by the sister for having been denied the same attention as the brother. This problem has recurred continually in psychoanalytic studies among Jews. It seems to be one cause for sibling rivalry that can be prevented effectively by providing the daughter with the same religious experience as the son. Furthermore, subconscious feelings of resentment against the religion will also be assuaged by according equal treatment to both sexes.

Summing up, the Bar and Bat Mitzvah ritual needn't be regarded as a superficial indication of Jewish survival *provided* that parent and child prepare well in advance of the ceremony to adopt a wholesome attitude regarding them. If added incentive can be provided to continue one's never-ending and fascinating spiritual and cultural development, then these ceremonies are worth every effort to retain them.

7

Sex Awareness Among Teenagers

Along with status and self-esteem, sex is the major preoccupation of teenagers. The awareness of one's own biological changes and those of the opposite sex during adolescence mark unmistakably this new stage in life. The preoccupation with members of one's own sex in the earlier years can no longer serve the emotional needs of the teenager. The adolescent possesses the procreative powers of manhood and womanhood, together with the urges and frustrations of adults which accompany these new forces.

Considerable teenage talk centers around sex. It is usually discussed within one's own age group, but often these days there is frank discussion with parents and teachers also.

Our teenagers do not mature physically earlier than they did in the past, but their curiosity is aroused at an earlier age than ever before. The entertainment media—movies, television, magazines, paperback book covers—arouse sexual impulses not only in adults and teenagers, but even among the pre-teenage group. Many anxious parents who are concerned about the time they should begin telling the children about sex all too often are astonished to learn that the youngsters have already acquired far more information, some of it distorted, than they ever had at a much later period in their youth. Many of the stories about youngsters in the position of teaching their parents about sex are not completely without foundation.

Parents should therefore have given up long ago the attempt to shelter their children from sex information. This delays the normal development of the child, and it also is a sheer waste of energy. Parental authority can never succeed in stemming the torrent of sex information so easily available to children today. Utter innocence may have been exalted and even attainable in other eras; today it is an impossible ideal to expect of any young man or woman who is not totally isolated from society.

It is, however, questionable whether parents should formally attempt to teach the child about sex unless the youngster is totally ignorant of basic sex information and has reached an age when such ignorance would be harmful. Parents may nevertheless answer specific questions with tactful frankness. The parent can above all impress upon the child that there is no need to feel ashamed of the parts of his body. God created our organs for specific functions. The daily Siddur contains a specific prayer in which we thank God for the body's organs which are indispensable to life. We needn't feel shame or guilt about anything that is part of God's design.

This does not mean that parents should encourage their children to succumb to their sex urges. Some fathers are unfortunately not reluctant to brag about the proven masculinity of their sons, and sometimes they encourage them to engage in premarital relations after being told "how to take care of themselves." This may well be a manifestation of the father's own secret desire for freedom and license, subdued merely by the restrictions that society has imposed upon him.

From a moral view point there can be no justification for a parent to encourage pre-marital sex indulgence by his son. The father should always ask himself, "How would I react if my daughter, rather than my son, were involved?"

It is quite understandable for us to expect that one's sex behavior before marriage should influence sex attitudes after marriage. Many men, it is true, who indulged in pre-marital relations, may have later settled down to a wholesome married life, but marriage is something more than a "settling-down" period. It is rather a period when the climax, the realization of one's hopes and expectations, is reached for the first time. The first profound sex experience if associated exclusively with marriage creates a unique bond between husband and wife who have patiently, though admittedly with difficulty, waited for the appropriate time to give themselves to each other in the spirit of genuine love. This memory of intimate communion shared for the first time in marriage strengthens the mutual relationship between them and renews itself with each recurring experience.

Victor Hugo wrote in this vein to his fiancée in 1820: "It is my desire to be worthy of you that has made me so severe on myself. If I am constantly preserved from those excesses too common to my age, and which the world so readily excuses, it is not because I have not had the chance to sin; but rather it is that the thought of you constantly preserves me. Thus have I kept intact, thanks to you, the sole treasures I can offer you on the day of marriage, a pure body and a virginal heart."

Young people in their conversations with one another have adopted several false notions about sex. Their reading has also given them distorted opinions on sex which may have never been intended by the authors they have read but who are nevertheless quoted to defend their views. Here are a few:

A—*Repressions and frustrations should be avoided.*

Young people with emotional problems are often advised to go out and express themselves sexually. After such experimentation, these young people have found that their unhappiness has become intensified, partially because they have been advised to seek relief *outside of themselves.*[1] Freud makes it clear that the problem of sex is one of adjusting tensions *within* the personality. The tension brought on by the sex urge, the social requirements pertaining to sex as the individual sees them, and the influence of moral training, all come together to form a complex problem and cannot be resolved by libertinism.

People tend to confuse the terms *repression* and *restraint.* By sex repression we usually mean more than abstaining from sex; we mean also the refusal to admit that we have any sex desire. Restraint or conscious self-control is altogether different. Repression is not healthy; self-control is. Pre-marital intercourse does not necessarily free us of repressions. It can often aggravate our problems because it can create feelings of guilt for having violated a moral code. It can also instill in us fears of pregnancy or disease.

Self-control is perhaps the great human trait unknown to the lower animals. If we were to surrender to all of our im-

[1] "To some extent it is a natural and normal form of overcoming separateness, and a partial answer to the problem of isolation. But in many individuals in whom separateness is not relieved in other ways, the search for the sexual orgasm assumes a function which makes it not very different from alcholism and drug addiction. It becomes a desperate attempt to escape the anxiety engendered by separateness, since the sexual act without love never bridges the gap between two human beings, except momentarily." Fromm, E., *The Art of Loving*, Harper and Bros., New York.

pulses and instincts, we could not live in peace with one another. There would be no morality, no family, no society.[2]

B—*Sex before marriage is educational.*

Some say that it helps us better to understand our anatomy and our physical needs if we determine by trial and error what we require in a husband or wife.

Experience has indicated that boys who engage in premarital relations are much too distracted to give thought to objective analysis. In most cases, they have confessed to counselors that they were preoccupied with the fear of being discovered. It is little more than an exciting emotional episode during which they are mainly interested in momentary satisfaction. The furtive planning before the act, the fear that parents or other adults will discover them, rule out the probability of any real educational value. Boys have compared the sex act to the sensation of quenching their thirst on a hot summer day—nothing more than momentary relief. For others, especially younger boys, it often leaves feelings of shame and self contempt which can understandably affect adversely their attitude toward sex for years and perhaps a lifetime.

As for girls, they generally admit that they don't even achieve a temporary satisfaction that the boys admit to. They will often feel resentment toward the boy for his lack of consideration and gentleness.

[2] Will Durant, addressing a high school graduation class in California, expressed these views about sex and the adolescent: ". . . . . Sex then becomes a fire and flame in the blood, and burns up the whole personality—which should be a hierarchy and harmony of desires.

Our civilization has unwisely stimulated this sexual impulse. Our ancestors played it down knowing that it was strong enough without prodding. We have blown it up with a thousand forms of incitation, advertisement, emphasis, and display, and have armed it with the doctrine that inhibition is a mistake—whereas inhibition, the control of the impulse, is the first principle of civilization. Don't let indoctrination determine your desires."

It may therefore be said that physical union before marriage is seldom a preview of sexual love after marriage. One cannot help but question its educational value.

C—Virginity is old-fashioned.

Even though many young people claim they would never want to marry a virgin, it is highly doubtful whether they are really expressing their genuine feelings. It is one thing to impress one's friends with an air of sophistication and another thing to admit our true opinion based on our religious, educational, and family background. Most young people have been taught explicitly, if not by inference, that sex before marriage is wrong. This belief has been instilled by family and community for so many generations that it has become deeply imbedded in our conscience. We may attempt to rationalize our disinterest in chastity, but we can't bury our conscience that easily.

Virginity can never be old-fashioned. Just as the institution of the family has weathered so many storms and has been challenged in so many new societies and has never been successfully replaced, so has chastity as an ideal never become obsolete despite the many attempts to discredit it.

The crux of the problem lies in the inability or unwillingness to look upon sex with sufficient reverence. What is meant to be sacred becomes profane. Sex becomes mainly a means of relieving tension, a proof of masculinity, a symbol of personal victory; it means acceptance by one's peers—everything but that for which it was originally intended.

Sam Levenson, the radio and television personality, expressed this very idea in a recent interview on "The Trouble with Teenagers." He said: "If you give a kid reverence, get him to feel that the moment of the creation of life is like the creation of the world itself, and that there is a tremendous responsibility in him for life. If you can teach him to respect life from a religious, cosmic, philosophic point of view, he ain't going to tamper with this thing so quickly.

"Life is a divine creation and if you can make a kid feel that this power is greater and more important than the girl he's got in the car for that moment, you've already created some kind of self-control and awe, and respect, a wonder which will stop him faster than all the simple little warnings you've given him."

The big problem is how parents can transmit this sense of reverence and wonder without losing the child's interest in the process of making their point. It is simple enough and perhaps more startling to tell the child about the dangers of pregnancy and all the social problems involved; but if this becomes the only reason for encouraging abstinence, then the child, male or female, will conclude that the way to combat the problem is by obtaining adequate protection.

The problem involves more than expediency. We are concerned with these moral and religious questions which parents should impress upon their children:

A—Unlike animals, human beings do not live solely for the present. We have the capacity to think ahead, to plan, to imagine the consequences of what we do today. Momentary satisfaction is often very costly if we look ahead months and years. We often live with a deep sense of guilt for taking advantage of another person's weakness. We lower their reputation in our own eyes and in the eyes of others—all because we may have acted on the impulse of the moment.

B—God has given us the power of creation. Among human beings this creative power should be treated with reverence. That is why there is a sacred marriage ceremony which precedes the sexual union of husband and wife. If this power is used before God intended, the marriage ceremony loses its meaning. It becomes more a jest than a religious ceremony.

I do not intend to enter into a discussion of the less intensive forms of sexual contact among young people other than to stress that there is a real risk in overemphasis on necking and petting, especially when they replace other means of communication between young people. When that happens they never obtain other information about each other. They may marry with the misconception that sexual compatibility is all that is necessary to live happily ever after—until they find out how wrong they were.

Boys and girls should learn about the value of simple, absorbing conversation. They should share similar hobbies and creative talents. They should be able to enjoy each other's company in a group. Dating entails far more than physical contact. It is one of the ways in which we learn how to get along with many people as well as with one person.

I know this is a minority opinion. Many teenagers will be unhappy with this point of view. Some will probably consider it to be no more than a pious wish of a prudish preacher. Many parents will consider the subject matter itself inappropriate for this book. "Let him stick to religion," they will insist. And as for the professionals, the psychiatrists and scientists who do not deal with value judgments in their work, this viewpoint may sound bizarre.

However, there is something else to consider. We have long been overly impressed with statistics. We have come to believe blindly that the practice of the majority, whether right or wrong, implies that the majority is correct. People tend to think that a Kinsey report is something more than a statistical study. It becomes also a guide for their own moral behavior. Little is said to counteract that notion. As the scientist insists on remaining objective, he is often content to describe situations as they are, without feeling the least obligation to depart from his scientific method.

When teenagers begin to speak freely, it is amazing how often they criticize themselves for doing what they feel the crowd impels them to do. Some confess that they can see no way to escape from the pattern. Girls in particular have painful conflicts. They want to be admired, to have dates, to be popular, but they may hate all that it involves—drinking and petting, especially with boys whom they dislike but who are also popular. Similarly, many boys in moments of frankness admit that they are not really "wolves" but that they have been caught in a web of conformity and didn't know how to escape the social aggressiveness of their companions.

The dangers of blind conformity have been stressed repeatedly in recent years, but usually without suggestions about combatting it. Parents, I believe, can deal with it constructively by emphasizing the fallacy of blind faith in statistics as a guide to correct behavior. If an average teenager in a survey gets the car so many times a week, watches television so many hours a day, and stays out until a particular hour on a date, it does not mean that such a pattern is necessarily good for our children. Similarly, if our neighbors are either too busy or too timorous to be concerned with their children's lack of standards in sex behavior, it does not necessarily follow that they should serve as a measuring rod for our family.[3] A parent who is genuinely concerned and ethically sensitive

[3] Joseph Wood Krutch in *Human Nature and the Human Condition* devotes an entire chapter to the common fallacy of overemphasizing statistics and averages. He claims that we have come to think of the average as normal. Contrary to popular opinion, "normal" is not a synonym for "average." "Mediocre," however, is a proper synonym. "And if we were accustomed to call the average man, not 'the common man' or still less 'the normal man' but 'the mediocre man,' we should not be so easily hypnotized into believing that mediocrity is an ideal to be aimed at." Krutch pleads that we return to the original meaning of the word "normal"—a rule or standard. A "normal man" would mean "what a man ought to be," which is different from the "average" or "mediocre" man whom we have wrongly regarded as most worthy of admiration.

realizes that he has a responsibility primarily to his own child, to help that child realize there is nothing sacred about being part of a majority when he, the child, believes the majority to be wrong. The child should also be taught an oft misunderstood lesson in democracy, namely, that the right to dissent is more important to democratic living than the necessity to follow the will of the majority.

8

Dating

If yesterday's generation of youth lacked seriousness, today it is criticized for being too serious, especially in its social life. It is not uncommon for a boy and girl of fifteen to decide that they are going steady. They are announcing to the others in their social world that they are henceforth unavailable and out of circulation. Even an invitation to the corner soda fountain or "cutting in" at dances by others is now frowned on. From the viewpoint of the teenager, going steady naturally has its advantages. No more worries for the girl about having to stay home over the week end; no more embarrassment for the boy in being refused a date because of a last minute call. There is also the matter of status. Boy and girl are both admired by their peers; they have gained a reputation for courage in having announced their intentions and for their maturity in having "settled down."

These crushes do not really resemble a love relationship because they do not involve to any great extent the happiness or well-being of the other person, but rather the extreme possessiveness of the subject who feels better if the object is possessed completely at all times. It is more an expression of the need for self-love.

Adolescent love relationships are frequently struck for no other reason than to relieve feelings of rejection, loneliness, and boredom. Anne Frank's relationship with Peter Van Daan was in some ways typical of teenage love. She recognized Peter to be "a rather soft, shy, gawky youth." She couldn't expect much from his company. Even though he was her senior by two and a half years, she realized that Peter was not mature enough to satisfy her emotional and intellectual needs. But most important, she was lavished with attention and regarded with sympathy; she knew that she could share her feelings with another young person. Her emotional needs demanded that she find a love object in Peter. She writes:

> My longing to talk to someone became so intense that somehow or other I took into my head to choose Peter . . . . . and the idea that I should beg for Peter's patronage was simply repellent. One can do a lot to satisfy one's longings, which certainly sticks out in my case, for I have made up my mind to go and sit with Peter more often and to get him talking somehow or other.

These infatuations in early adolescence are usually short-lived. A disagreement, a newer or more exciting friend, can dissolve the former romance as rapidly as it developed. But with each love affair many family conflicts can, and do, arise. Not all parents are amused by serious dating in early adolescence. They are disturbed by the lack of concern their children show for their school work and, even more, the lack of attention that they as parents are receiving. There arise new conflicts over money, and over the family car, and there are the seemingly endless hours of telephonic trivia.[1]

[1] Dr. Gerald Pearson in his *Adolescence and the Conflict of Generations*, W. W. Norton, N. Y. 1958, analyzes these prolonged telephone conversations in this way: "The adolescent's ego feels weak and helpless. He tries to strengthen it by forming close relationships with one or more other people,

The "arranged marriage" of another era has been vanishing, particularly in the West, and it is not likely to return. That does not mean, however, that parents should play an inactive role in the social life of the child. Parental wisdom, growing out of experience and concern, is essential to counteract the distorted emphasis on romantic love as the sole basis of marriage. Who more than parents understand the needs of their children? Who more than parents must mend the broken marriages of young people?

The results do not speak well for the judgment of young people who insist on early marriage and living as they please. According to the 1958 United Nations Demographic Yearbook, 22.5 per cent of divorced women were 24 or under, and 24 per cent of those divorced had been married less than two years. One out of every twenty divorced women now remarrying is a teenager.

How can parents lay the groundwork for more active participation in the choice of their child's partner? They should begin conditioning their children toward good marriages at a very early age by emphasizing that man and wife have more than a responsibility to themselves. Marriage has long-lasting consequences. It produces children who have to be reared, children who become the society of the future. The strength of a nation, as Carle Zimmerman of Harvard has pointed out, closely parallels the solidarity of a family system.

Parents should freely discuss their own marriage realistically with their children, and these children will take seriously the reasons for its relative success or failure.

---

by having an ideal or best friend. These people are not love objects—regardless of the similarity or difference in sex—but are objects for identification. The extended telephone conversations serve the same purpose; it is as if all separation between the two persons is avoided through the use of the telephone. . . . The adolescent wishes the other person to be himself and he to be the other person, so that instead of his ego's feeling weak and helpless, it will feel stronger because of the addition of the other person's ego."

Unfortunately, parents who are attempting to guide their children into sound marriages are not getting the support of considerable public opinion which tends to regard parental interference with young love as old-fashioned meddling. Even in school many teachers often destroy the parents' authority by discussing marriage as a union between two people in love who should learn to become personally compatible. According to Dr. A. H. Hobbes, the most popular textbooks in marriage preparation emphasize romance and individuality, and de-emphasize the crucial role of marriage in creating the next generation.

Parents are certainly within their rights in requesting their teenage children to expand their social contacts rather than to concentrate on one particular boy or girl at an early age. In spite of the advantages felt by the child in going steady, he can be made to understand the importance of availability to others who seek his friendship. We are inclined to close our minds precisely at that stage of life when we should be most curious. We should seek a variety of personalities during the adolescent years from which our concept of the ideal husband or wife will eventually emerge, for it is only through trial and error that our tastes become more defined. It must also be pointed out that this is the time for concentration on studies and for serious deliberation in career planning.

Young people should be encouraged to make acquaintances with all kinds of boys and girls, with a variety of personalities, so that they themselves become better balanced personalities. You cannot learn to appreciate the classics if you spend all your leisure time reading comics. Varied types of people bring out new qualities in us, including many qualities we were unaware of previously. Why should we limit our acquaintances at such an impressionable age? [2]

[2] Dr. Gerald Pearson in *Adolescence and the Conflict of Generations* finds that diversified social experience in adolescence helps the youngster in his

Young people who choose to go steady are also limiting the time they can spend with friends of their own sex. Their schedule becomes so concentrated on one person that they deny themselves some of the cherished opportunities of give and take that a group of girls or boys have among themselves. The bull sessions and the small talk play an important part in child development, but a young couple going steady may not be very tolerant of these activities that take them away from one another.

Parents may indicate that sexual desire is naturally heightened during prolonged intimacy, and that it can almost effortlessly lead into a complete sexual relationship. Self-control becomes more and more difficult, demanding unusual strength and self denial. Constant restraint can also have undesirable consequences, making both boy and girl irritable and quarrelsome with one another and with their parents. For this reason, among others, many sensitive people who do not want to do the wrong thing decide on an early marriage before they are prepared for it emotionally, socially, and financially.

It should be emphasized that going steady in itself is not immoral. Many happily married couples were childhood sweethearts whose genuine love for each other blossomed and matured over a period of many years. But children should not be shielded from the possible consequences that may follow from such a decision.

We are fully aware that a child in his early teens who has decided to keep steady company will not readily respond to

---

struggle to achieve a personal identity. "Therefore, the seemingly polygamous matter of the fickle adolescent simply represents a trial and error learning process of consolidating his ego by the incorporation of a number of apparently divergent ideals. Adults who did not have any temporary love affairs during adolescence are compelled to seek them in adult life; this often has quite grave consequences, for adult love affairs are more serious and are experienced not by a developing personality, but by one whose development is somewhat fixed."

rational argument against such a course. He is too emotionally involved in his personal accomplishment to be swayed by cold logic. Sound arguments nevertheless have a way of penetrating, even though this is not evident for some months, but perhaps in time for the second "love affair."

Parents should by no means attempt to shame the child out of going steady by deriding their daughter's boy friend or their son's girl friend. Nor should ridicule of the child ever be the parent's weapon. The most effective method for creating bitterness and resentment is ridicule. Attempts to interfere with a child's privacy by prying into diaries or opening letters or by demanding a detailed description of each date or party are all self defeating. All these are supposedly done for the teenager's "good," but they indicate an unconscious resentment against the child for simply growing up.

Tact and patience are essential in dealing with the delicate problem of inter-dating. Parents are here challenged by their children to show them why they should not date anyone of any religious faith whose company they enjoy. In America today most of the barriers that once separated Jew and non-Jew have been broken down. Jewish children of today don't even understand the meaning of the word "ghetto" unless it has been explained in a particular historical setting. One of the outstanding features of the public school system is the opportunity it affords to all Americans regardless of religious affiliation to work and play together, to learn that there are more factors uniting than dividing us. And have parents not stressed to their children all these years the equality of all people? Have they not been impressed with the idea that it makes little difference what the religion or color of other children may be, that they are as good as we are?

But suddenly the parents seem to arrive at a new theory: that others are not good enough for us. We must build barriers all over again now that we have been successful in helping to break them down. This attitude is difficult to understand even for many children who live in large cities where Jewish associations are numerous, where there are synagogues and community centers in which Jewish children can meet. But when parents impose these restrictions in a small town, it can also result in self-imposed social ostracism. How, then, are we to deal with the dilemma?

There appears to be a fine but real distinction between socializing as a group and socializing as individuals. To attend a class function or a school dance or to invite schoolmates to a party at home is not at all the same as intimate dating between two individuals. Not that there is anything intrinsically immoral about inter-dating. It is rather a self-written invitation to possible involvement that could lead to intermarriage. We may wish to point out to our children that once the habit of inter-dating is acquired, it becomes gradually easier to accept intermarriage as normal. Like paper which folds more easily every time it is creased, so it is with human habits once begun.

Many a young person who has insisted that he would never marry someone out of his faith eventually became so emotionally involved that no argument seemed reasonable enough to prevent intermarriage.

The age of dating is pleasant and joyous. It is also a serious period of one's life. It is the time of sifting, when we learn to recognize those qualities in the other sex that best complement elements of our personality. Actually we begin planning for marriage much earlier. Little girls become conditioned to motherhood from the time they begin to fondle and care for their dolls. Boys who sell papers and magazines, mow the lawn and run errands, learn the value of money and are preparing for their role in married life many years before they are expected to support wife and children.

In discussing inter-dating the problems that occur with

intermarriage could be pointed out to the adolescent. There are some successful inter-marriages, but we should remember the many obstacles that threaten the chances for a happily married life. A recent study of 12,000 people in Maryland indicated that where both parents were Protestants, 6.8 per cent of the parents were separated; and for Catholics it was 6.4 per cent. Where there was a mixed marriage the divorce rate was 15.2 per cent; and where there was no religion it was 16.7 per cent.[3]

First, the difference in background often creates severe conflicts in married life. Even in families where either or both parents received a meager religious training, they retain some beliefs and behavior patterns which are an inextricable part of their personality structure. When two people are very much in love, they minimize these differences, insisting that the things they hold in common are much stronger than their diverse backgrounds, but after marriage, when the first stage of romance gives way to the realistic problems of raising a family, they become conscious of religious experiences in childhood, and are anxious to transmit them to their children.

It is then that the question of religious education takes on great importance. Should not a child belong to some religious group? If he has not been given a background or some instruction in any religion, the child is incapable of making a wise choice himself, since choosing a religion requires far more than the capacity to make a spontaneous decision. Only after one has lived in a particular religious environment can he wisely decide if he wants to accept or reject it. It is not at all like making a choice between purchasing one of two commodities. And if the parents decide to wait until the

[3] National Jewish Monthly, (April, 1959) *Is Inter-Marriage Inevitable?* by Joseph Rosenblum.

child becomes an adult before he need make a choice, they will during that period be denying him that which is almost as basic to a child's security as the need for parental love. In spite of the fact that a parent may choose to disavow any religious affiliation, to do so places the child at a decided disadvantage. He is unable to identify himself along religious lines in a way that other children do. He feels a sense of loneliness and rejection, since he is not anchored in a particular religious tradition. Must the child be saddled with these problems that shortsighted parents impose upon him.[4]

Besides practical considerations, there is also an ideological question. Is a Jew not as responsible for the future survival of his people as a citizen is for his country? Is a man who renounces his tradition not like the soldier who chooses to desert his comrades when all available men are needed? Experience has shown us that in most cases of intermarriage, the Jewish partner bows to the religious preference of the non-Jew. In Washington, D. C., for example, a study has revealed that 11 per cent of the Jewish families have intermarried partners. In 66 per cent of these families the children were not being reared as Jews. In 25 per cent, they were. In 9 per cent, one child was being reared as a Jew while another was not. Commenting on this study in the 1958 American Jewish Year Book, Alvin Chenkin states: "The evidence seems clear that intermarriage, in its long term results, represent an 'invisible loss' to the Jewish community."

[4] "Nothing could be more mistaken than the common parental attitude that formal religious affiliation should be deferred until the child is "old enough" to make his own decision. This attitude is encountered especially often in interfaith marriages. To defer affiliation until the school years or adolescence is to by-pass an important developmental phase in the life of the child; it has unfortunate effects, not only on the problem of personal identification, but on other psychological problems as well. *Our clinical data indicate that parents should make the decision for the child and make it before he has reached the age of five.* Linn, Louis, M. D., and Schwartz, Leo. *Psychiatry and Religious Experience,* Random House, N. Y. 1958.

This same view point has been stressed by our students of Jewish history. For example, Professor Salo Baron of Columbia University noted: "In the majority of cases, mixed marriages result in the abandonment of the Jewish creed by the partner. Even where an actual change in religious allegiance fails to materialize, mixed marriages are seldom prolific, and their offspring for the most part join a non-Jewish creed or at least become professed agnostics. It is mainly for this reason that even Reform Judaism combats intermarriage." [5]

Unfortunately, parents do not always employ tact or sound reasoning in airing their views on inter-dating. The parent who prefers "any girl so long as she is Jewish," cannot expect a sympathetic response from her son who feels that he is worthy of a girl with character and that being born a Jew doesn't automatically instill character.

Let parents also remember that they cannot effectively appeal to their children by simply pointing out how the neighbors and relatives react to his dating patterns. This is basically a parent-child problem. The child can usually be made to feel sympathetic by a sincere and reasonable objection by parents, but not because of the reactions by uncles and aunts, friends and neighbors.

For this reason Judaism should mean more to parents than maintaining a biological kinship. We all know that too many parents are more concerned in keeping Jews together as a group, but have little interest in Judaism. Their children are probably well aware that there is no such thing as Jewish blood or specifically Jewish racial characteristics. Parents who have for years had no sympathy for Jewish traditions and who have not maintained any religious affiliation cannot expect to present a convincing case against inter-dating or intermar-

[5] Baron, Salo. *A Social and Religious History of The Jews,* Volume 2, Columbia University Press, 1937.

riage. Children are quick to recognize a sudden and insincere spurt of Jewish interest as a last ditch attempt to avert the problem. Why, even parents who have given the child positive values from infancy are not always certain whether the child will be strong enough to resist his impulses when faced with a test. But there is at least a more favorable chance if some inner direction has been supplemented with wise parental advice. What, then, can the formerly apathetic parent expect if the long-devoted parents can only *hope* for the best without ever being certain of the outcome?

Just as proper food and wholesome recreation, though essential to the physical well-being of the child, cannot assure good health in later life, since so many complications may appear with the maturing body, so are we uncertain about the social outlook of the child in his maturing years despite the prolonged, concentrated, devoted efforts of the parent. But who will deny that parents must make a genuine effort to at least minimize such possibilities by providing in childhood the best care and concern of which they are capable.

9

Meeting Prejudices

Prejudice is known to start at an early age, long before adolescence. Arnold Gesell reports that even four-year-olds sometimes exclude other children. A bigot may well be in the making by the age of six or seven, when racial name-calling is not at all uncommon; at eight, clubs may be formed which will exclude members for racial or religious reasons only. But for the most part early forms of prejudice are merely verbal, and even then the name-caller is not fully aware of the significance of his words. He may use the term "Jew" without knowing its meaning, simply repeating a phrase that he has heard from older children, or from his parents who may have referred to Jews without any malicious intent.

It is during adolescence, however, that prejudice may have serious implications. A child of fourteen or fifteen is prepared to defend his views and to take action against those whom he feels are unworthy of his friendship. He will embark on a campaign of slander. He will resort to malicious methods of exclusion. He may even attempt to "fight it out," provided he is confident of winning. In some overcrowded city areas in particular, where neighborhood gangs still roam the streets, racial and religious hostility manifests itself by physical violence against "intruders."

In today's suburbia, where a more cordial relationship is said to exist among all religious groups, prejudice less frequently takes on the form of physical combat.[1] Nevertheless inter-religious tensions are present in the suburbs. I have addressed many teenage church groups at which I have welcomed the opportunity to discuss frankly their own non-Jewish attitudes toward their Jewish friends and neighbors. The most frequent questions asked were:

1—*"Why do the Jewish kids stick so closely together?"*— They questioned the need for high school fraternities and sororities and expressed the feeling that their Jewish friends went out of their way to associate with their own group even during lunch and recess periods. When asked if they were aware that they were excluding Jews by forming their own groups, they answered no. But Jewish teenagers have told me in similar informal discussions that they were seldom made to feel welcome by their non-Jewish classmates and were merely reacting to Gentile exclusiveness.

2—*"Are there any poor Jews?"*—This was a common question. They also wanted to know if Jews ever make a living by working with their hands. Both are ancient questions about Jews and have been current for centuries. In the past, however, these were accusations rather than questions, and that makes a vast difference. Nevertheless, they do reveal a profound ignorance about Jews by well-meaning non-Jews who judge them by the relatively few they meet as neighbors or in business.

[1] For a comprehensive study of Christian-Jewish relations in suburbia, see Albert Gordon's *Jews in Suburbia*, Beacon Press, Boston (1959) Ch. 7.

3—*"Why do Jews seem to live so ostentatiously?"*—They seem disturbed that their Jewish friends liked to brag about their homes, their cars, and their television sets. Even though some of the other non-Jewish participants refuted these accusations, the questioners still felt that their Jewish friends liked to show off.

4—*"Why don't Jews believe in the divinity of Jesus and accept the New Testament?"*—The majority did not believe that the Jews killed Jesus, but did feel the Jews were partially responsible for his death. It was difficult for some of the youths to understand why Jews were still "holding out." A few referred to the United States as a "Christian country." Most of them did not see anything wrong with Christian missionaries among the Jews, but admitted that they would resent Jewish missionary activity among the Christians.

5—*"Why do Jews create religious tensions in the school?"*—They referred specifically to the objections of Jewish parents and children regarding Christian celebrations in the public schools and required attendance at the baccalaureate services. Most of these students were not in the least acquainted with the principle of separation between church and state and even after it was explained to them admitted that it had little meaning for them.

Although communication between religious groups helps to minimize some misunderstanding and lessen tensions, there nevertheless remain deep-seated prejudices that persist even after many friendly meetings. The most skillful teacher cannot successfully eradicate negative attitudes built up in the home over years and generations. Parental superstitions and antagonisms are transferred to the child in the most devious ways. Many studies have revealed, for example, that in a home where parents are exceedingly harsh, suppressive, or critical, the child is far more prone to manifest prejudice against other groups. He is on his guard. He learns that authority rather than trust and tolerance dominates human relationships. He learns to distrust himself, and through the simple act of projection, he comes to fear evil impulses in others: "They have evil designs and are not to be trusted."

The child who feels secure and wanted usually develops a healthy attitude toward equality of all men. He is more inclined to place his trust in most men. Not required to repress his own impulses, he is not likely to transfer them to others, nor develop superstitions and fears.[2]

Eric Fromm differentiates between two kinds of hate, rational and irrational. Rational hate is a person's reaction to an actual threat to his own or another person's freedom, life or ideas. Irrational hate, with which we are here concerned, he calls "character-conditioned."[3] It is often a gratuitous hate which has little relation to reality, although it may be the result of many disappointments in life. A person must hate *something*. Finding a victim of hatred gives him a feeling of relief as though he were happy to have the opportunity to express his lingering hostility. The roots of this hatred may baffle him, but he must find some convenient target and some good reason—e.g. the Jews are conspiring against him or plan to take over all the businesses in the country.

How can parents effectively gird their adolescent children with self-confidence against such acts of prejudice? More important than the problem of the existence of anti-Semitism,

[2] Gordon Allport in his *Nature of Prejudice* (Doubleday Anchor, 1958) records that certain seriously maladjusted children whose difficulty stemmed from an insecure home life showed open sympathy during World War II with enemy countries and turned against America and its minority groups —especially the Jews.

[3] Fromm, E., *Man for Himself,* Rinehart, New York, 1947.

which perhaps may never be completely eradicated, is the manner in which the Jew learns to react to it. There are many possible approaches, but not all of them face the problem realistically.

It has been suggested by some authorities that the child be made aware at an early age that he is a member of the less privileged minority group and that he must accept this fact sooner or later. Professor Kurt Lewin was a strong advocate of this approach. He claimed that parents should avoid the soft approach even in an environment where the child does not encounter prejudice in his early life. "Parents should realize that the problem is bound to arise at some time, and the sooner it is faced the better." [4]

Such an approach may have been adequate for a child brought up in an East European environment or in Germany during the thirties. But is it not self-defeating to ask a child to accept an underprivileged role in a country that guarantees all men first-class citizenship? American Jewry accepts this land as its home and professes to know no other. The rights and privileges of Jews, as of all other groups, are guaranteed by law. The American nation is basically decent and fair. Why, then, train our children to continue to accept the stigma of a persecuted minority?

There are others who contend that the solution of anti-Semitism lies in our showing the non-Jew that we are not at all what they think we are. Their children are told that through concerted Jewish good-will efforts a solution to bigotry can be found. But should this burden of peace-making be placed upon us and upon our children? Must the victims of prejudice continue to make a fetish of good-will when there must exist a mutual interest in overcoming bigotry? Our cooperation in good-will efforts is essential, but when planning programs

[4] Lewin, K., *Resolving Social Conflicts*, Harper & Bros. N. Y. 1948.

with teenagers, one hears repeatedly that the Jews should initiate the brotherhood programs and interfaith services.

Still other teenagers seem convinced that the solution to the problem of discrimination lies in forming their own in-groups. Jewish High School fraternities and sororities prevail in many communities and apparently are not discouraged by the parents. These groups, unlike the United Synagogue Youth, AZA or B'nai Brith girls, are committed to no Jewish programming. They are primarily non-sectarian groups with social objectives. However, not only are non-Jews refused membership, but Jewish youngsters who do not meet their sometimes arbitrary standards are similarly excluded. One cannot help but seriously question the effectiveness of these social groups despite their popularity on the American Jewish scene, and despite their efforts in combatting the problem of discrimination against Jews. One wonders whether fighting social exclusiveness with our own exclusive measures is the answer. When Jews exclude other Jews from Jewish organizations, they are agreeing, in effect, that some Jews are unworthy of associating with them. Is this so different, then, from the policies of some clubs which practice Jewish exclusion?

How, then, may parents effectively prepare their children against prejudice?

A—There is no valid substitute for a sound Jewish education as a most effective weapon against bigotry. As mentioned previously, it is doubtful whether prejudice can ever be eradicated even in an enlightened environment, since there are so many hidden factors causing fear and suspicion of minorities. But youngsters can learn to be on guard against the rantings of the anti-Semite once they learn to accept themselves unequivocally as Jews. The marginal Jew becomes far more disturbed by prejudice than the secure one whose pride cannot be easily deflated by irresponsible attacks. The ancient Hebrew sages described this value of Jewish education when, commenting on the famous line from Genesis, "The voice is the voice of Jacob and the hands are the hands of Esau," they exclaimed that when the voices of children can be heard in the halls of Jewish learning, then the hands of Esau—the enemy—can never destroy them.

Knowledge of Jewish history can help to bolster the morale of young people who are confronted with anti-Semitism. They will learn that accusations against Jews date back to the time of the Pharaoh who invented the idea that Jews would be disloyal in times of war. They will learn also that Haman was incensed with Mordecai and his people because they were different—the oft-repeated problem of dislike for the unlike. The student of history soon discovers that anti-Semitism is irrational, that it is the product of a diseased mind which always seeks an object of attack. The bigot will seek out the most convenient and helpless target. Those who have been deprived of studying Jewish history may have difficulty in contesting the bigot's accusations. Some Jews without a sound background in history may even feel they should share the guilt of their forebears for being Christ-killers or for choosing to be money lenders when other choices were open before them.

Rabbi Milton Steinberg, who was recognized as an outstanding analyst of Jewish problems before his untimely death, wrote: "And because my Jewishness is something positive, anti-Semitism looms less large in my life than in that of many of my fellows. I am not hag ridden by it as they are . . . . and I know that while much will be taken from me in the event of my defeat, my Jewish heritage will still remain to sustain and give me direction. The de-Judaized Jews on

the other hand recognize quite clearly that they will be left
with nothing. Little wonder that their preoccupation with
anti-Semitism approaches a hysteria." [5]

B—Our young people should be taught to regard their
minority status as a privilege. The fact that we represent 4
per cent of the total population of the country does not place
us in an unfortunate position. We are one of the many minorities whose influence reaches far beyond mere numerical
strength. As a religious community, American Jews are considered one of the three major groups in this country. We are
represented, along with Protestants and Catholics, at affairs
of State; we are consulted with them on important problems
dealing with the national and community welfare.

The Jews have suffered more than other minority in the
history of mankind, and yet our minority status has at the
same time placed us in a most strategic position in which we
have been enabled to teach mankind some of its most important lessons. We have shown the way by defying every au-
thoritarian government that demanded absolute conformity;
we have prevented the enduring success of dictators by insisting on our right to be different. Only recently Soviet
Premier Nikita Khrushchev admitted that the Jews in the
Soviet Union were too individualistic.

Because of its individualism, this unique minority served
constantly as a gadfly, a ferment in convention-bound society.
The Jews have often encouraged other minorities to refuse
regimentation as too high a price for mere physical protection.
The Jews have often sounded the alarm for small and great
nations, warning them that once the bigot attacked the Jew
he would then turn his attention to the devastation of other

[5] Steinberg, M., *A Partisan Guide To The Jewish Problem*, Bobbs-Merrill,
Indianapolis, N. Y., 1945.

people and finally the bravest citizens of his own country.

But perhaps most important of all, the Jews have demonstrated to the world that, given the will to live, one's spirit need never be broken. No method of torture has ever subdued the Jewish soul. The fire of the Mosaic faith has melted the most lethal weapon set upon Jews throughout history.

For these and other reasons too numerous to mention, our young can be taught that to be a member of this minority is to wear a badge of honor.

C—Another method of instilling pride and self confidence in our Jewish youth is by inculcating in them a love for Zion. No event in the past two thousand years has had a greater impact on Jewish morale than the establishment of the new state of Israel. Young and old alike cannot but be impressed by this modern day miracle in which the American Jew has played a major role.

Any visitor to Israel would find sufficient reason to take pride in the immense accomplishments of the land since 1948. He would see for himself how the many myths invented about Jews centuries ago have been exploded. Jews are not parasites; they are skilled soldiers; they can till the soil; they can work skillfully with their hands. No work in Israel is too menial for them. They cannot be stereotyped. Jews do not look alike, nor do they think or act alike. Liberals and conservatives, capitalists and laborers, the bearded and the clean-shaven, are all working together to create a permanent home for themselves and for their children.

By arranging for their children to visit Israel for a month or a year, American parents can sometimes do more to bolster their Jewish morale than years of continued explanation and discussion can accomplish here.

Keeping in mind the irrational nature of prejudice, one

cannot emphasize enough that to dissipate one's energies in trying to eliminate the source of dissatisfaction will not only result in wasted effort, but, more important, the Jew will lose his self respect in the process. To steer clear of community activity because Jews are accused of being too aggressive will produce the accusation that Jews are not interested in community matters and consequently do not make good citizens. To refrain from running for political office because a few people say that a Jew seeks to control the government is tantamount to self-incrimination. To take seriously taunts about Jewish liberalism by deciding to withdraw from liberal movements will not even begin to placate the anti-Semite.

We must not permit ourselves ever to leave any legitimate business or profession to which we are dedicated. Anti-Semites have been known to speak with exaggeration of the Jewish monopoly in the motion picture and clothing industries. This is all the more reason for Jews who happen to be in these occupations to remain there. Not that these occupations are necessarily better than others, but Jews must learn to reassert their rights when they are challenged.

H. C. Engelbrecht, writing with deep conviction and understanding, offers this advice: "The first and most important thing for Jews is not to be driven into an attitude of retreat. Never back up! Never trim your sails to the poisonous winds of anti-Semitic detraction! Do not permit the vilifications of Jew-haters to rule or determine your lives. Above all, avoid by all means the Ghetto mind—cringing before slander, fawning before ignorance, taking on protective coloration!" [6]

Our youngsters should be adequately trained to differentiate between actual and doubtful incidents of prejudice. We often become ultra-sensitive to remarks that are not at all based on anti-Semitic feelings but are rather expressions re-

[6] *Opinion,* 1937.

flecting ignorance or immaturity. We must not see provoca-
tion where none has been intended; we should give the man
suspected of bigotry the benefit of the doubt and not miscon-
strue the meaning of isolated incidents or chance remarks
taken out of context. When we are convinced that we are
dealing with unmistakable anti-Semitism, we ought to use
every legitimate means available to combat it, keeping in
mind that it is a responsibility we owe to ourselves and to
others, Jews and non-Jews alike.

Young people have often become convinced that a teacher
who has given examinations on Jewish holidays is prejudiced
against Jews. Their parents have supported their conviction
without inquiring whether the teacher was even aware of the
problem. Similarly, not every job refused a Jew is based on
discrimination against all Jews. It may pertain to personality,
to skill, talent, competence, a variety of factors in no way related to race or religion. The anecdote about the stutterer
who was refused a position as radio announcer because he felt
the employer was anti-Semitic reflects an all-too-common unwillingness to admit that often the problem lies within one-
self. It is when a bigoted pattern is repeated or when chance
remarks are followed by prejudicial action that there is little
alternative but to take appropriate steps and to deal with the
bigot from a position of strength.

It should be understood that Jews who expect fair treatment should carefully examine their own prejudices. Parents
should guard their remarks in private and in the presence of
their children. If they happen to hear their youngsters depre-
cating non-Jews, they should explain immediately that those
who want the respect of others must give those others equal
respect. Being part of a minority group does not confer exclusive rights or privileges upon its members.

Finally, a wholesome training in the home can most effectively help the child withstand anti-Semitic attacks. That is the great and historic preventive of Jewish life and history. Positive Jewish experience for the child in the home in the early years should be valued more than spending one's adult life combatting anti-Semites. We should first convince ourselves and our young that Judaism has something to offer us before we can convince our neighbors that Jews have something to offer them.

Part II
What They Are Asking
About Religion

What They Are Asking About Religion

Now that we have discussed the development of parental approaches to teenage problems, we move to a more specific area, namely, general questions about religion and particularly about Judaism that perplex our young people. All of the questions presented in this section have been asked either by the teenagers themselves in group and private discussions or by their parents who reported their children's questions to me.

The reader will note that almost every question is phrased negatively, and that could easily give the erroneous impression that religious skepticism is the predominant mood among teenagers today. To repeat, this is not so. We should keep in mind that young people will often instinctively ask questions in a skeptical tone in order to elicit a positive reply which will fortify their innate beliefs and opinions. They would be sorely disappointed to receive an equally negative response. Furthermore, these have been selected from hundreds of other questions, most of which required factual rather than attitudinal answers and were therefore not included in the scope of this volume.

There has been no intention to include more than a sampling of questions asked by Jewish teenagers; neither are the answers intended to be exhaustive. They represent one of many approaches to particular problems and not necessarily *the* answer. Indeed, no one can provide *the* answers to matters of Jewish belief, since Judaism cannot be reduced to a pat formula or catechism. Though attempts have been made in the past to formulate a set of Jewish dogmas, there was never unanimous agreement on the dogmas to be accepted. Some distinguished scholars forcefully argued against the very existence of Jewish dogma.

I have not planned to cover the field of Jewish theology in this section, but rather to include some of the religious concepts that pertain to Jewish adolescents. There is, however, an extensive literature to which the parent can turn for further information even though it is merely touched upon here because of space limitations.

I know my answers here are not always objective; at times they may even read like part of a sermon. I have discovered that in spite of every effort to avoid the temptation of preaching in writing such a book, the nature of the questions has evoked an emotional involvement in which objectivity could not be maintained.

The questions addressed to the parent may be phrased quite differently than here, and the answers will often vary and should be adjusted to the youngster's Jewish background and intelligence. The answers are not primarily intended for the youngster, but are for the use of the parent so that he, the parent, may equip himself to discuss these religious questions with greater self-confidence. By so doing he will encourage the child to seek further knowledge.

Question.   Is it sinful to have religious doubts?

Answer.   No sensitive person goes through life without questioning his faith in God. One finds much injustice in the world. Innocent people become the victims of poverty, disease, and war. Unscrupulous people frequently enjoy ill-gotten wealth and even live to a ripe old age. All of us occasionally become skeptical in the face of such glaring injustice.

Whether doubting is sinful depends therefore on the nature of one's doubts. If we are looking for religious faith, but find it occasionally difficult despite our sincere searching, then such doubts cannot be considered sinful. The Bible contains many examples of heroic personalities who at times expressed doubts about God. Tradition does not look unfavorably upon Abraham the Patriarch because he questioned God's justice in wanting to destroy the people of Sodom. Even Moses, whom our tradition reveres as the master of prophets, had moments of serious doubt when called upon to speak to the Pharaoh. The author of the Psalms on occasion voices a note of skepticism when he complains: "Lord, how long shall the wicked exult?" Ecclesiastes, who chose wisdom as his guide, had difficulty resolving his doubts. He considered man no better than the beast and his end the same. What he really questioned was the traditional belief that man was created in the image of God, and yet the Book of Ecclesiastes was included among the sacred books of the Bible and is still read in the synagogue on Sukkot. Apparently our sages understood our natural inclination to question and did not fear an occasional lapse of faith. They expected us to resolve our doubts eventually because they felt that man yearns above all for faith in God and that he who seeks it earnestly enough will ultimately find it.

Unlike the Biblical personalities who sought faith but may

have lost it temporarily, there are people who want to doubt, and constantly seek ways to fortify their skepticism. They close their minds to debate lest they become convinced that their doubting is unreasonable. These are the same people who on a rare occasion come into the church or synagogue with a defiant attitude, as if to say, "Convince me, make me believe," when in reality they do not want to be convinced at all.

Even a person undergoing surgery should agree to the need for an operation by becoming mentally and emotionally prepared before he is placed on the operating table; otherwise, the most skillful surgeon may not succeed with his task. Similarly, one should be receptive to faith when he attends a service, listens to a sermon, or reads the Bible. Otherwise he will probably not be convinced that he should believe.

Hence, any person who consciously closes his mind to new ideas, whether they be social, scientific, or religious, is sinning in the larger sense because he refuses to use the intelligence with which he has been endowed.

*   *   *

Question. Isn't religion a personal affair that exists between man and his conscience? What difference, then, should my belief make to other people?

Answer. This opinion is only valid in part. True, our religion is a personal matter in that no one can tell us how to believe. We should not be expected to reveal our religious beliefs when applying for college entrance or for a job. Neither is a public servant who is running for political office expected to divulge his religious convictions. Otherwise our whole democratic structure would be threatened. People would come to vote on a basis of one's religious association or theological beliefs and not on competence or experience.

A member of a religious minority would have little chance of election to public office.

But there are times when one's religious beliefs are of concern to others and not merely a matter of personal conviction. When young people are contemplating marriage they should openly discuss beforehand their religious beliefs. If emotional, physical and intellectual compatability are deemed important, so is religious compatability. A man who will refuse to join a synagogue after marriage in spite of the woman's interest in Judaism, and a woman who refuses to keep kashrut in a home where the man has never eaten non-kosher food are both inviting serious difficulty in their married life.

Because many people are convinced that religion is a personal affair, they sometimes resent any influence that may be exerted upon them to change their beliefs. But persuasion is used in many other areas of daily life. Advertising attempts to persuade us to buy certain products. Unsavory methods are often used to persuade the public to buy this or that brand of toothpaste, cigarettes, or detergents. Unfortunately, there are too few people who have protested against such brainwashing methods in modern advertising. Now, when a rabbi or layman is convinced that faith in God, prayer, or even Sabbath observance has great value for the individual Jew and for the survival of Judaism, their honest efforts should not be resented, especially since there is no profit motive involved here as in advertising.

Young people who are preparing to enter college should be informed in advance that they will be confronted with many conflicting philosophies and points of view. Their instructors not only teach their particular subjects but frequently attempt to "sell" their religious, political, and social beliefs. Even a mathematics or science instructor who is supposedly devoted to the objective search for truth often discusses his agnostic or atheistic views in the classroom. These conflicting viewpoints are not necessarily harmful to the student. The student's capacity to absorb these various points of view is necessary to his mental growth and development. But along with the other philosophies, the positive religious viewpoint should also have a hearing in this great marketplace of ideas. Otherwise the student's alternative may be seriously limited; he will not have the opportunity to choose between a positive and negative religious belief.

Every person has a religion of some kind. If it is not good religion, it may be bad religion. If it is not God-centered, it may be a religion where materialism (the god of success), Communism (the god of power), or hedonism (the god of pleasure), is considered the highest good. Why, then, should the student be exposed solely to these philosophies and God-centered religion kept under lock and key because it is too personal a matter to discuss in public.

It is taken for granted that we are living in a voluntary society where no one can or should want to control the religious beliefs of others. We all have the right to practice as little or as much religion as we choose or, for that matter, no religion at all if we so decide. We cannot force others to renounce their Jewish identification if they refuse to expose themselves to the religious influence of the synagogue. But they should not resent the efforts of those who are seriously concerned about the religious apathy of their fellow Jews and attempt to remedy the situation.

*   *   *

Question.   Why must I believe in God in order to live a good life? There are many people who live by a moral code and yet do not have faith in God.

Answer.   It is true that some people do live by a strict moral code, and yet they *claim* that they do not believe in

God. Others profess to be believers, but their actions indicate that they have no faith. To *claim* belief means nothing at all unless one attempts to live up to the moral standards that his religion requires.

We should keep in mind that many of these ethical disbelievers are not conscious of their faith in God because they are confused about the meaning of faith. They can't believe in the God that they knew as children and have failed to develop a more mature concept of God.

These moralists, who claim to have no belief, are still largely influenced by religious ideas, and the religious people with whom they associate. They are products of a basically religious civilization. Would they be as moral were they isolated from the influence of religion? Will their grandchildren, coming from a totally irreligious household, continue to live by a moral standard without religious influence.

Sincere belief in God can help accomplish the following:

A—It can teach us that goodness is not a "take-it-or-leave-it" affair, necessary for some but not for others. The religionist believes that laws against stealing, cheating, or slander were divinely ordained. They should be followed by all people who want to live a decent life and contribute to a moral society. The disbeliever who chooses to live a moral life may not agree that such a code of moral behavior is necessary for people who choose to live otherwise. He may excuse the unsociable genius or the non-conforming artist who sets up his own ethical code.

It is not difficult to understand what dangerous results can come from such a flexible moral attitude where each man chooses to live by his own code of ethics.[1] We have seen what

---

[1] Joseph Wood Krutch, analyzing the problem of moral relativism, writes: "The pure relativist who denies the existence of *anything* permanent in human nature and who then finds himself shocked by, let us say, the 'atrocities' committed against the dead by Nazi authorities, is logically bound to tell himself that he is merely reacting according to a prejudice unworthy

has happened in our own country in recent years when a group of people claimed they could interpret the Constitution in their own way even if it meant the defiance of Supreme Court authority. The same disorder would exist if men defied the moral authority of God by interpreting it as they saw fit.

However, when men agree that there is a higher authority than themselves to which they as human beings are subject, then they feel the responsibility to live up to God's ethical requirements as found in the writings of the great religions. Just as in military life, there must be one commander-in-chief in order to prevent anarchy and disorder, so should the ethical standards set by religion be accepted by all men for the same basic reason.

B—Faith in God also encourages us to live a good life not only when it requires little effort, but also under the most trying circumstances when it may become inconvenient or unpopular to do so. Albert Einstein observed that in Nazi Germany it was not the scientists nor the college professors to whom the victims could turn to for help, but rather to the devotees of religion whose faith did not fail them even in time of great personal danger.

It was this abiding faith in God that gave our Jewish forbears the strength and character to choose goodness simply because God required it. Without faith they might have chosen the easier path of surrender, but at the expense of succumbing to evil.

*   *   *

---

of one who has come to understand intellectually that custom is never more than custom and that there is no reason why, for instance, corpses should not always be made into useful soap—as they were in Germany during the second world war.

Human Nature and the Human Condition, Random House, 1959.

Question. **Am I on safe religious ground if I believe in God as an idea or symbol?**

Answer. It is natural for people to look for certainty. Because of the influence of science in our lives, we are not content to accept that which cannot be classified or defined. But let us remember that when we reduce God to a pat formula, we fail to grasp His infinite character. Furthermore, we make ourselves omniscient when we claim that He is nothing more than an idea or a symbol that we create.

By reducing God to an ideal or symbol which we can fully understand in a literal sense we rule out the necessity for the concept of faith from which religion receives its greatest sustenance. We have faith God exists; we assume God exists, and it is this wonderfully elusive quality of God that gives meaning to religion. Remove the mystic element from religion and you rob it of its vitality. You make it a mere science, and it is infinitely more than that, as it must be to sustain us effectively.

Furthermore, how are we to believe in prayer and its effectiveness if God is nothing more than an idea or a symbol? Is prayer nothing more than a simple resolution on our part, such as bouncing a ball against a wall and then catching it ourselves? Unless God personally reacts and is moved by men's prayers, then worship is nothing more than an exercise in autosuggestion.

To worship a "symbolic" God is a distortion of religion, for we do nothing more than create a useful or convenient picture of Him in our mind and worship our symbol, just as they do who have created visible images for the sake of convenience. What difference does it make whether the symbol is visible or invisible? If we are the creators of a god *idea* or *symbol,* then we should call it by another name, such as the

Good or the Ideal but not God, which means something more profound to those who believe in Him.

Abraham Heschel in his *Man's Quest for God* poses the question in this way: "If God has no mercy and offers no light to those who grope for Him, does He deserve man's efforts to reach Him? . . . . and just as he who loves a person does not love a symbol or his own idea of the person but the person himself, so he who loves God and fears God is not satisfied with worshipping a symbol or worshipping symbolically."

*   *   *

Question.   Did God create man or did we create Him?

Answer.   We have come a long way through the years in developing a more mature understanding of God to meet the demands of our intellectual growth. Even in the Bible we detect that Moses had a clearer grasp of God than the patriarchs. The prophets, in turn, contributed further toward a more mature understanding of God, and so have we moderns benefited from the intelligence of each generation. In similar manner future generations will know more about God than we do today. The modern sciences, unknown to the ancients, have given us new insights about God and religion as well as the mysteries of the physical sciences.

We say in the Amidah "the God of Abraham, the God of Isaac, the God of Jacob," and not God of Abraham, Isaac and Jacob. This indicates that Isaac and Jacob did not merely take over Abraham's conception of God. Each found in Him even more, and each added his own understanding to that which he had learned from a previous generation.

Commenting on God's utterance at the burning bush, "I shall be what I shall be," the rabbis explain that there is no fixed idea that all generations must have of God. The future tense is used to show that the concept of God is inextricably related to the stage of civilization that men continue to attain with the passing generations.

This does not suggest, however, that God did not exist before man discovered Him, just as it cannot be implied that atomic energy was non-existent before modern man discovered it.

When youngsters grow into adulthood and have their own families, they often begin to realize for the first time how wise their parents had been over the years. The parents have not necessarily changed, but the youngsters assuredly have. Emotional and intellectual maturity now enables the adult to discover qualities in his parents that always existed. It is, then, in maturity that God is no longer an imaginary being or a convenient symbol invented by some ingenious person or group who needed an object of worship, but rather a Power whose existence is independent of man.

*   *   *

Question.   **If God is invisible how can one picture Him?**

Answer.   The Talmud relates the story of a pious man who was singing the praises of God. After he had finished, a rabbi asked him: "Did you list all the praises there are? Have you exhausted the subject?"

"No," replied the man.

The rabbi then said: "When you added adjective upon adjective and finally stopped, you implied that you had finally exhausted them. Isn't it better, therefore, not to use any adjectives at all?"

Since God can never be adequately described, we can best define Him by stating what He is *not*. God is not a person, He has neither shape nor form, He is incorruptible. By giving a positive description of God we limit Him because we endow Him with human qualities.

And yet, knowing that we can never adequately envisage God, man craves to have a convenient "picture" of Him. Jewish tradition does not forbid us to envisage God in a particular way as long as we understand that our knowledge of Him is limited and that our envisagement is symbolic, not literal. It may be compared with looking at a map, when we must understand that we are not seeing countries, cities, and states as they are, but rather are seeing the convenient symbols that represent vast areas.

Milton Steinberg once wrote that when he thought of God and His relationship to the world he imagined a mighty river with currents, waves, ripples, and bubbles. Each current, wave, ripple, and bubble exists independently, yet each is part of the stream and is carried along by it in its course. Furthermore, there is more to the river, depths below depths, than is visible to the eye.

So do all things stand in relationship to God. Each has its independent existence, yet each exists only because of God moving with His purpose. "Touch anything and you may say: 'He is here.' Yet add all things together and you will not have Him, for He is more than the world."

Another scholar conceives of God as an unseen friend who whispers in our ear and tells us what is right and wrong. The emphasis in this concept of God is that primarily he is our conscience urging us to follow the right and avoid the wrong path.

I myself regard God as an all-consuming fire. Every human being possesses a spark from that fire: the soul. Though the flame gives off numerous sparks, its strength and brilliance are not diminished in the least by its giving. When man dies, this divine spark returns to its original source. Knowing well that God's essence and our relationship to Him do not fit this description, it is nevertheless helpful to envisage Him in terms of a parable or symbol.

*   *   *

Question. **If man is so insignificant when compared to God, how is any knowledge about Him possible?**

Answer. No man will ever discover all that there is to know about God. Even Moses, the greatest of our prophets, possessed a very limited knowledge of God. "No man shall see Me and live," say the Scriptures, meaning that no mortal shall ever know all about God.

However, some extraordinary people do know more about God than others by virtue of the special moral and intellectual powers with which God has endowed them. Just as we have our geniuses in science and the arts, so do we have geniuses in religion, men who are in closer contact with God than those who are not so endowed.

The prominent Jewish scholar, Robert Gordis, suggested the following analogy in his book, *Judaism for the Modern Age.* Imagine a group of people in a room and someone addresses them. The average person will grasp his conversation without difficulty, but these same people would be unable to detect the radio waves that are present in the same room. Then a boy brings an inexpensive radio into the room and now the group may hear the sounds coming from powerful transmitting stations. Yet the sound waves of distant or weaker stations will still not be heard until a more sensitive radio is produced. All the sound waves are in the same room, but their reception depends on the various instruments attuned to them.

Our capacity to grasp God's word depends on the degree

of receptivity within us. Those with extraordinary insight can grasp more of the divine truth than others. In no case, however, will the human mind grasp precisely what comes from the source. We expect some degree of distortion of the original sound, but the finer the instrument the higher the fidelity.

*   *   *

Question. **How can a person stricken with illness be expected to have faith in God?**

Answer. People often make the mistake of believing that God causes or wills sickness. Perhaps we need a more mature understanding of how He functions in our lives. People are not stricken with disease because it is God's will. God assumes the responsibility for the creation and development of the vital organs comprising the human body. Sometimes these organs become diseased and fail to function properly. God does not remove these organs nor does He change their function, just as He does not change the properties of water in which a man may be drowning, even though water is the immediate cause of possible tragedy.

Joshua Loth Liebman writes in his *Peace of Mind:* "When God made water He endowed it with the properties of floating ships and turning mill wheels. These are accounted good. But in the very nature of water is its inherent capacity to drown us. And so it is with all other laws of nature—in their very orderliness is the guarantee that God is. That orderliness, however, limits the range of His whim and caprice."

God, then, is like an architect who provides the blueprint, the pattern, which makes human life possible. Man is like the builder who then proceeds to implement the pattern or design of the Divine Architect. It is understandable that disease and illness will appear in humans, none of whom is phy-

sically perfect. It is surprising, if not miraculous, that so
many people enjoy good health despite the complex makeup
of the human body and the ills to which it is always exposed.

No, God did not complete the process of creation. He makes
human creation possible and implants in us the wisdom which
can bring this creation closer and closer to perfection. When
men of science engage in medical research and physicians
heal the sick, they fulfill a divine task in helping to complete
"the unfinished business" of creation. Mankind needs to be
challenged. Without the determination to overcome obstacles,
man would have little opportunity to use his divinely endowed skills and to fulfill his human talents.

The theory that God created an incomplete world is not
new. We read in the Torah: "Because in it [the Sabbath] He
rested from all His work which He created *La'Asot* (to do)."
An ancient sage noted that the text does not read *V'Asa*, "and
which He made," but *La'Asot*, "yet to do," to teach that
"there is yet more work to be done."

*   *   *

Question.   **How can God be interested in us as individuals?**

Answer.   This question is basic not only to Judaism, but
to all religions. The validity of prayer hinges on the problem
of God's interest in individuals. If God is merely an impersonal Power or Force, then He cannot react to our prayers;
on the other hand, if He is concerned with us as individuals,
then prayer has meaning.

Our major difficulty in believing that God is interested in
individuals lies in our tendency to compare Him with ourselves. Because we tend to personalize, we find it impossible
to imagine that God can remember so many names and faces.

We cannot even properly begin to conceive of God unless we free ourselves of the notion that our natures are alike.

That God knows and is interested in each individual is the subject of much discussion in Jewish sources. The Palestinian Talmud states: "If a man sees crowds of men he should repeat the words: 'Blessed is He who is wise in mysterious things,' for as the features of no two are alike, so the thoughts of no two are alike." If God has created every person differently, it is conceivable that He could be acquainted with his individual traits.

The Reverend Ralph Sockman, writing on this problem, answers the skeptic as follows: ". . . Love has a way of individualizing, irrespective of numbers. Though there may be ten children in a family, the parents know the peculiar qualities of each. If a child dies, the father does not dismiss the matter lightly because he has lost one-tenth of his brood. In the home each member is a person, not a percentage. And if earthly fathers thus individualize their children, who can set limits to the infinite love of the Heavenly Father?" [1]

If we are able to believe that God implants a soul within each human being and that that soul is the divine in man, then we can imagine the possibility of God's concern for the individual and His interest in each human being. God is looking after His investment and His share in man, so to speak.

* * *

Question. **Is belief in God not a matter of blind faith?**

Answer. Although many people have attempted to prove God's existence by means of logic, it cannot be done. Man must supply another ingredient in his quest for God and faith in God. This does not mean that our search for belief should rest on blind faith which is contrary to reason, but that it

[1] Sockman, Ralph, *How to Believe.* New York: Doubleday, 1953.

should go further than reason alone can carry us. Those who have blind faith are not interested in the reasonableness of their faith. They would believe in Him even if their reason would disprove His existence.

With some believers, faith in God is arrived at first, after which they discover why their faith makes sense. With others, faith in God comes only after they conclude His existence is a reasonable assumption. According to our tradition, faith came to Abraham only after he had surmised that the sun, the moon, and the stars which he saw as divine manifestations could not possibly be divine in themselves. His faith in an invisible God came after more searching investigation. But it makes little difference in which order faith comes to an individual so long as it does not discourage his search for a reasonable proof of God's existence.

Briefly, why does God's existence appear reasonable even though we cannot prove it as one proves a mathematical equation?

A—*The harmonious beauty of the world about us* startles even the most casual observer. In spite of its size, everything in the world appears to be interrelated, fitting into a unified pattern. The world of nature is well-ordered and governed by law. Electrons and protons, plant life and animal life, all behave in harmony with their nature; their behavior is predictable; law prevails everywhere.

B—*The world of nature is largely purposive;* even the lower forms of animal life appear to be working toward a goal. An insect lays eggs in a particular place so that the unborn larvae will have sufficient food to survive. The spider weaves its web for a particular reason. The bird builds its nest with purpose.

Animals are born with means of protection for their survival. The bat is equipped with natural "radar" in order to fly safely in darkness. The toad can better escape from intruders with his protective coloration. The skunk relies on his ability to give off an unpleasant odor as his means of protection. The theory of evolution, far from minimizing God's role in creation, points clearly to purpose and design in nature. If man has evolved from the lower forms of life, as the modernist contends, then there is good reason to believe that a supreme Mind was responsible for this upward development.

C—*The mind and consciousness of man* offer a reasonable argument for God's existence. In addition to his animal instincts, man uniquely possesses intelligence, a thirst for truth, beauty, and goodness. Man's awareness of himself and his potentialities and his ability to conceive of God's existence, give encouragement to the believer.

D—*The course of history,* which appears to follow a pattern and purpose, also gives rise to the belief that God's influence has been present. That smaller nations often prevailed over stronger ones because the former were more ethical may be attributed to God's influence in the shaping of history. The ability of the Jewish people to survive throughout the ages, defying the opposition of the strongest nations, stirs one anew to faith in God's existence.

These are only a few of the many factors pointing to the reasonableness of faith in a Supreme Being.

*   *   *

Question. Why must one be required to fear God? We cannot love a person or being that we are expected to fear.

Answer. We are not required to fear God in the same sense that people fear a tyrant or dictator. The term *"yir'at hashem,"* which is usually translated "fear of the Lord," actually implies respect or awe before God. It also implies a sense of wonder before the mysterious ways of God which are unknown to man. It is true that we cannot love that which we fear, but we can love that which we respect. Where there is no respect, love cannot exist.

Why is this idea so important in our religious thinking? Because when man has no feeling of respect for others, he makes his own rules; he becomes capable of committing any wrong that he can get away with. Not so the man who respects the wisdom and experience of others, such as his parents and teachers. It is through respect for them that he learns to curb his selfishness and vanity.

Once he has learned to respect other humans, he can begin to grasp the meaning of respect for God. He learns that just as his parents are good, God too represents *Perfect Goodness;* just as his teachers are wise, God represents *Perfect Wisdom.* He learns that even the greatest of men owe respect to God and are guided by His will because all goodness and wisdom flow from Him.

Though the "fear of God" should be understood in terms of respect for Him, the fear of sin should be taken more literally. One should fear sin as he fears sickness, disease, or warfare. It is the fear of their consequences that arouses us to resist them. When our fathers approached the Days of Awe with "fear and trembling," they feared the sins that they had committed, but not God whom they were assured would forgive them and love them. They feared their own moral weakness. They feared the possibility of the evil in them taking over and becoming master of the good.

For us, too, a healthy fear of sin can stimulate the good to control the evil.

*   *   *

Question. **Can one deny the existence of God and still remain a Jew?**

Answer. There are Jews who profess atheism and yet are not excluded from being Jews. Besides being born of Jewish parents, many of them want to be regarded as members of the Jewish people. They may continue to work for Jewish charities or help promote Jewish cultural interests, and yet they have no direct affiliation with religious institutions.

It does appear a bit strange that the Jewish people, whose origin, history, and survival have been so closely linked with religion do not require religious belief in order to remain within the Jewish fold. However, one should understand what the term "Jew" implies. The Jews are a people, essentially religious, but not exclusively so. Its members have many things in common—their religious beliefs and practices, their culture and history, an ancient tradition, the common language of prayer, and their determination to remain a people.

Now, if a Jew who does not share in the religious beliefs and practices of Judaism still wants to continue his affiliation with the Jewish people by identifying himself with only some of their common experiences, his affiliation will not be denied to him.

Whether he is realizing the most that such an affiliation can offer is questionable. Just as a member of an organization who may be interested only in a limited part of its program does not genuinely enjoy its full benefits, so does the non-religious Jew deprive himself of the most vital aspect of Jewish people-hood—its religion. Primarily because of their religion, the Jews achieved the status of a people and managed to survive throughout the centuries. Their vast culture, their stirring history, their love of Zion—all are replete with religious inspiration and content. Religion has been the soul of the Jewish people.

The eminent Jewish thinker, Mordecai Kaplan, includes in a broad definition of religion and religious people, many who do not consider themselves to be religious. "All who are interested in Jewish civilization and want it to help them achieve a life that is worthwhile for themselves and for others have a share in Jewish religion. They may not think of themselves as religious. That is because they identify religion with some limited or mistaken conception of it. Yet, in so far as they do help the Jewish People make of its civilization a source of salvation for themselves, their fellow Jews, and mankind, they really practice Jewish religion even though they do not call it such." [1]

*   *   *

Question. Why must we pray in a synagogue to be reminded of God? Many people feel closer to Him when they are surrounded by nature than in a house of worship.

Answer. There are many people who claim that they feel closer to God when they are surrounded by the wonders of nature. The patriarch, Isaac, felt the presence of God out in the field. Moses was overcome with religious feeling when he saw a little bush. Beauties of nature should inspire us to feel a nearness to God, but they cannot serve as a substitute for a house of worship.

A person may feel a religious experience when seeing a beautiful sunset, but the question remains: What does that feeling do for him? Is he merely left with a warm sensation, permitting it to become extinguished after he leaves the scene of beauty? Furthermore, the experience of beauty does not alone stimulate morality and the pursuit of truth. Experience has shown us that we need to be reminded constantly of what we feel to be good and true. Providing us with these reminders is one of the main functions of synagogue worship.

[1] Kaplan, M. M., *Questions Jews Ask: Reconstructionist Answers.* N. Y.: Reconstructionist Press, 1956

Our dedication to righteousness is enhanced if we repeat again and again important prayers, or if we listen to the reading of the Scriptures week after week. These repetitions do not allow us to forget the values we hold dear. It is so easy to take them for granted, to overlook them because of our frail nature.

Even with the help of reminders provided by the prayers and ritual objects in the synagogue, we often forget their meaning. How much more forgetful would we become without them?

It is true that there are many non-synagogue Jews who are highly ethical people. Many of them, however, had been consciously or unconsciously influenced by the atmosphere of the synagogue in their youth. Many prominent men who may now feel little necessity to participate in public worship spent many hours in the synagogue during their most impressionable years. These people seldom ask themselves what their own lives would have been like were they denied this experience. It is highly questionable whether the wonders of nature alone could have influenced them to abide by a strict moral code.

Dr. Elton Trueblood regards this viewpoint as the "angelic fallacy," and he continues as follows about the man who holds it: "He makes the mistake of supposing that he and his fellows are angels, when, in reality, they are men. If we were angels it is doubtless true that we should not need the external support which institutionalized religion gives. . . . . We might then worship as well by the seaside, among the hot-dog stands, as at the altar. But we do not happen to be that way."

*   *   *

Question. **Hasn't the overemphasis on sin driven many people away from religion?**

Answer. Undoubtedly the emphasis on sin has kept people away from involvement in religion. Few people are willing to admit to themselves or to others that they are sinners; moreover, they are frequently confused about the meaning of sin. Why should one live with feelings of guilt when he can avoid contact with the church or synagogue which hinders his freedom and reminds him of his shortcomings?

One reason why psychiatry has appealed to so many modern people is that it attempts to avoid use of the word "sin." A person who constantly errs may be compelled to do so by causes beyond his control, or he may be emotionally disturbed, but he will not be accused of sinning. Archibald Macleish in his award-winning play, *J.B.*, has the psychoanalyst exclaim: "Self has no will, cannot be guilty." He says to Job: "There is no guilt, my man. We all are victims of our guilt, not guilty."

In recent years many religious leaders have come to recognize sin in a different light. They now recognize that error or rebellion is not always sinful, especially where inner compulsion is the cause. At the same time, the religionist feels that man usually has the freedom to avoid repeating errors by following the good path. When we are in control of our thoughts and actions and we fail to exercise mastery over ourselves, then we are sinning. Blaming mother, father, or society at large for our sins is a mark of cowardice. We should be able to face up to our own shortcomings; otherwise we will never seek self-improvement.

In the past, many religious thinkers confused the people by calling any violation, whether of a moral or ritual nature, a sin. Though we believe that following the rituals will benefit the individual and the group, failure to observe them does not necessarily constitute sin. We sin when we ignore or violate moral laws, as, for example, when we steal, gossip, or dishonor our elders. To call both riding on the Sabbath and stealing sinful is not only confusing but also unrealistic.

To be sure, there are some ritual laws which, when ignored completely, do constitute sin. Riding on the Sabbath in itself may not be a sin, but if the Jew completely ignores the Sabbath, treating it as any other day in the week, he is saying in effect that he denies God's role in the creation of the world.

Similarly, if a person does not pray on a particular day, he has not committed a sinful act, but if he ignores prayer completely or scoffs at it, he then refuses to recognize his most important means of communion with God, which is tantamount to saying that he does not need God at all.

To understand the nature and consequence of sin and to strive toward its eradication are perhaps the most important functions of religion.

*   *   *

Question. **Why must miracles play such an important part in our religious belief?**

Answer. It is true that the Bible records many examples of miracles. The ancient mind found little difficulty in believing that an all-powerful God would suspend the laws of nature.

In the Talmudic era, however, the rabbis were concerned with the whole problem of miracles and sought explanations for them which satisfied their critical minds *and* their faith in the Bible. They believed that during the creation of the world, when natural law was ordained, God provided for miraculous departure from it. "Ten things were created on the eve of the first Sabbath of creation at twilight." This category includes such miracles as Balaam's talking donkey, the manna, and the rod of Moses. The belief in angels was seriously questioned by no less a figure than the great Rabbi Judah the Prince.

The Talmud states that a prayer for God to change events which have already taken place is a "vain prayer." If a man's wife is with child and he says, "May it be thy will that my wife shall bear a male," this is considered a useless prayer. If a man is returning from a journey and hears a sound of lamentation in the city and says, "May it be thy will that they who lament be not of my house," this is a useless prayer.

In the Middle Ages, Maimonides, the greatest Jewish mind of the period, reinterpreted some of the miracle stories in Scripture. Though he could not deny resurrection of the body, his medical background and scientific mind would not allow him to accept the then common notion that the body would exist forever. He taught that the people of Israel did not believe in Moses because of the miracles he performed, but because of what happened at Mount Sinai, which was not a suspension of the law of nature.

Unlike Christianity, Judaism does not depend on a particular miracle; without such a miracle, the whole structure of Christianity would crumble. Our loyalty to Judaism does not depend on the acceptance or rejection of the miracles related in the Bible, but on the religious and moral requirements that the Bible imposes on us.

At the same time, it would be illogical to rule out the possibility of miracles altogether. Dr. Warren Weaver, one of the country's distinguished scientists, approaches the question of miracles in this manner:

"Put a kettle of water on the stove. What happens? Does the water get hot and boil or does it freeze? The nineteenth-century scientist would have considered it ridiculous to ask the question. But scientists today, aware of the peculiarities of modern physical theories, would say, 'In the overwhelming proportion of the cases, the water will get hot and boil.' But in one of the vast number of trials, it is to be expected that the water will freeze rather than boil. . . . No one can logically hold that science rules out miracles as impossible." [1]

This may well be our attitude toward miracles. To accept them all as literally as they are related in the Bible is to surrender reason. To reject them all as being impossible even by God is to surrender faith.

Moreover, even those people who deny that nature's laws have been or ever will be suspended cannot be called unbelievers. Many of them hold that God causes extraordinary natural events to occur, events which seemed impossible at one time but have since occurred. To place an artificial satellite in orbit around the sun, to reestablish a homeland after nineteen hundred years of exile, are both natural miracles even though they are not a suspension of nature's laws. Both would have been called impossible one hundred years ago.

* * *

Question. **Why does a scientist devoted to humanity need religion?**

Answer. Today, as in the past, there are scientists who feel they have no need for religion. They often look upon religion as an obstacle to scientific advancement and sometimes seem to say, "Why must I be expected to believe in a God when I can't begin to understand what God means? It was because of religion that people resisted and fought the proven theories of Copernicus, Galileo, and other men of science." Even more sympathetic scientists, who agree that religion helps humanity, claim nevertheless that they are

[1] Rosten, L., *A Guide to the Religions of America.* New York: Simon & Schuster, 1955.

benefiting mankind in their own way and do not require religion for themselves.

It is true that followers of religion have not always been sympathetic to scientific progress, but it is not the fault of religion that people misuse it. Religion serves a different purpose than science and at the same time is needed to complement science. The scientist is trained to deal with the *quantitative*, or that which is measurable. Anything that cannot be measured is not pertinent to his work because it cannot be controlled scientifically. The religionist, on the other hand, is interested mainly in the *qualitative*. He deals with ideas and values which are as real to him as any object that can be put into one's hand or tested in the laboratory.

The scientist must not approach his project with preconceived notions. He must be thoroughly impersonal and factual. The religionist, however, is personal in outlook. He is emotionally involved in his subject. Joe Smith cannot be merely labeled *genus homo sapiens,* for he is an individual with feelings and emotions and with unique qualities of character.

Both religion and science need each other. Science seeks to answer the question "How?" How can we get man to the moon? How can we prolong life? How can we best detect cancer?

Religion, by contrast, grapples with "Why?" in man and in human history. Why do the righteous suffer? Why is it better to follow truth than falsehood? Why must we work for universal peace? Mankind wants and needs answers to these questions. The scientist cannot well afford to ignore the questions that religion asks outside the laboratory, just as the man of religion depends heavily on the findings of the scientist.

Scientists are human beings above all. They have their periods of stress and fear. They require warmth and love, and they are also expected to give these to others. They want to be treated with respect, just as they are expected to respect others. Any man, whatever his occupation, who feels that he is above these human needs, is either deceiving himself or is more a robot than a man. Religion aids in rounding out this personality by helping us deal more effectively with our fears, our moral problems, our relationships with our fellow men.

*   *   *

Question. **Why can't an artist find in his dedicated way of life a valid substitute for religion?**

Answer. Art is by no means foreign to the Jewish religion. The Biblical artist, Bezalel, is regarded with great reverence as a man filled with divine inspiration.—"And I have filled him with a spirit of God, in wisdom, and in understanding, and in knowledge, and in all manner of workmanship to devise skillful works, to work in gold and in silver and in brass." (Exodus 31:2, 3). Even though the absence of images or pictures is conspicious in the synagogue, lest they become objects of worship, artistic expression has not been prohibited. God is pictured in Jewish tradition as the Artist of artists.

Yet, art is by no means a substitute for religion. The artist does not necessarily feel the need to be virtuous, nor must he be concerned with the needs of others. He requires no plan, as a rule, by which to aid society, although art has sometimes helped to uncover tyranny and falsehood. The artist is frequently an individualist who wishes to remain aloof from organized movements devoted to communal and world problems.

By contrast, a man of religion feels the necessity to speak out on social issues, for he is usually group-minded. He is anxious to help society by calling others to action. He creates and supports causes, organizes groups, and insists on moral solutions to social problems. He has a world viewpoint, whereas the artist who is devoted to his limited work often has none. Where the artist may be unwilling to commit himself by passing judgment on great social issues, since he is often content to depict things as they are or as he alone sees them, a man with genuine religious belief must go further in concerning himself with things as they ought to be, as God would want them to be.

Religion then is hospitable to art. It needs art to give it added beauty and poetic expression, but it does not follow that the artistic life requires no other disciplines.

*   *   *

Question.   **Why should I believe in prayer if the prayers of so many people obviously go unanswered?**

Answer.   People often expect God to do their work for them. They pray for certain things and then sit back and wait for results. As one person phrased it, God is regarded as the "cosmic bellhop" who should respond rapidly to our command. Jewish tradition teaches that man and God are partners. If we desire something, and our desire is legitimate, then we must show enough interest in our petition to work toward that goal. God, we believe, responds to our interest and our action.

God cannot be expected to respond to man's whims. To anticipate His help to win a basketball game or to improve our appearance, as important as these may be to us, is not a legitimate request. God alone is the true Judge who decides what prayers are worthy of being considered.

We often think that God has not answered our prayers when in reality he has answered us in the most unexpected ways. We may not even be aware that He is responding to our prayers, for His ways of doing things are totally different from ours.

Contrary to popular opinion, the highest purpose of prayer is not to ask God to serve us, but rather to inspire ourselves to serve Him and thus come closer to Him. Shneur Zalman was once overhead saying: "I do not want your Paradise, I do not want your world to come. I want You and You only."

Prayer is also expressed in gratitude to God for the things that we have already received. When a person can sincerely say, "Thank you, God," then he is humbly recognizing his dependence on God for the gifts of life. He knows that he is not a "self-made man" but that he has been the recipient of God's blessings.

It is surprising to observe many intelligent men and women, some of whom have gained considerable intellectual eminence, admit that they do not pray because God did not answer their prayers in the past. This reflects an immature approach to or even the fetish concept of religion. George Foote Moore in his classic work, *The Birth And Growth Of Religion,* describes a very primitive practice which many moderns have still not outgrown. He writes: "The fetish is treated with respect, since the spirit in it might resent being otherwise treated. The owner talks to it, cajoles it, tells it what he wants and expects of it. If it does not work he upbraids it, and if it continues to disappoint him, he throws it away. . . ."

People who have attained success also need prayer. They forget the function of prayer in their lives. Besides expressing gratitude, a man of wealth has reason to pray that he use his money wisely and for the greatest good. A teacher has reason to pray that he be able to impart his knowledge effectively to his students; a scientist could pray that his discoveries be used to *help* human beings and not to *hurt* them.

To obtain the true value of prayer one should be content to experience the rich spiritual reward of feeling closer to God. If material reward comes to him, let him accept it with humble gratitude and surprise, but let him not pray with this condition in mind.

*   *   *

Question. **Don't the practices of different religions divide groups? How can we hope for one world if each group insists on its own practices?**

Answer. To expect everyone regardless of origin to follow one religion is as impracticable as the desire to have all people dress alike, eat the same food, or speak the same language. Men cannot be expected to forget their history and culture and to sever their connections with the past, especially if that past has not outlived its usefulness.

There are indeed some people who feel that a single all-embracing world religion would help to eliminate war and strife. Even if one religion were attainable, it is questionable whether this would help to solve the problems of humanity. If greed and hunger for power have caused brothers in the same family to war with one another, why should we expect one religious faith to accomplish more?

People who look upon theirs as the only genuine religion are doing a great disservice to humanity. Similarly, people who regard the observance of their religious ceremonies as an end in itself sever themselves from those who are unlike them. But when these ceremonies are thought of properly as means of expressing a universal ideal, then one cannot help but feel a brotherly bond to men everywhere.

Consider the Sabbath. Its observance has helped to unify the Jewish people throughout the ages. It has strengthened our Jewish identity. But the Sabbath has also a universal social message to impart. Its meaning is directed to all people who must have regular periods of rest. It says in effect that employer and employee alike need the opportunity to refresh themselves physically and spiritually at least once a week. Even animals should not be worked incessantly. The social implications of the Sabbath for humanity should never be overlooked.

Rosh Hashana is observed by Jews only, but its meaning is universal. Its observance serves to solidify the relatively small Jewish group, but it also helps to closely identify all Jews with the entire human race which, according to tradition, came into being on this day. We read on this holiday the magnificent prayer commencing with these words:

> *And all the world shall come to serve Thee*
> *And praise Thy glorious name*
> *And Thy righteousness triumphant*
> *The islands shall acclaim.*

The dietary laws too may be peculiar to Israel, but they teach us to have regard for all God's creation, even animal life.

Jewish ritual is a particular way of dramatizing a universal ideal, and for that reason it is necessary to keep in mind the meaning behind the ritual and acquaint ourselves with its underlying value. God is not satisfied to have us perform these rituals mechanically or to consider them as ends in themselves, but as means for achieving noble ends.

*   *   *

Question. How can I accept religion when I read of all the atrocities committed in its name?

Answer. It is true that for centuries people have continually used religion as a convenient excuse for committing crimes. Wars have been needlessly waged because "it was

God's will" to annihilate the enemy. Segregation of races has been advocated in the name of the Bible. Segregationists have cited the Bible as the authority for proving that God Himself dispersed the races after the attempt was made to build the tower of Babel. People have refused to accept medical aid for themselves and their children because it was against their religious convictions. Progress in science was impeded because it was deemed against God's will to disturb the order of nature.

But must we place the blame on religion because people misinterpret it? Can we justly deny the need for religion because some people have sought Biblical approval for their prejudices? By taking words out of their original context, one can find support for any cause one chooses. The Constitution, the Declaration of Independence, the Bill of Rights, can be misinterpreted in similar fashion if people are not sincerely interested in being guided by their true meaning.

Looking upon religion as the culprit brings to mind the discussion between Gamliel and the philosopher. The philosopher asked: "If there is not usefulness in the idols, why doesn't your God destroy them?" To which Gamliel replied: "Is it only one particular object that you worship? Look, you worship the sun, moon, stars, planets, mountains, the hills, the springs, glens, and even human beings. Shall God destroy the world because of fools?" But again the philosopher persisted: "Since the idols according to you cause the wicked to stumble, why does not your God remove them from the world?" To which Gamliel again replied: "But human beings are also worshipped and shall God destroy the world because of fools?"

As the quality of a tree is usually judged by its best fruit, so should religion be judged by the great personalities who have been influenced by its principles. If we fail to accept this premise, then we should be consistent and judge all disciplines and institutions by those who have abused them. We should then judge the value of nationalism not as it was interpreted by Thomas Jefferson but by those who exploited it for selfish ends, such as Hitler and Mussolini.

In order to defend the integrity of religion, we must understand just what the religious sources originally intended, what was the background, what were the special circumstances and the peculiar environment out of which emerged certain Biblical passages. We should not ask that God's will as revealed in the Bible should conform with ours, but rather to discover what His will really is and then strive to make our will conform with His.

*   *   *

Question.   How does the observance of rituals make one a better person?

Answer.   Unquestionably the mechanical observance of ritual does not make one a better person. God is not in need of our ritual observance; however, we are in need of rituals, for if properly understood and observed rituals can help train us in the development of character and self-discipline. As Rav taught, "The *Mitzvot* were given only for the purpose of disciplining and refining men through their observance."

We do not know the particular reasons why many of the *Mitzvot* have been prescribed, but experience has taught us the value of their observance.

A: Rituals have taught Jews the necessity for moderation and discipline. Man's natural impulses if allowed to go unchecked could serve evil consequences. It is a *mitzvah* to eat, but not excessively. Likewise, we are exhorted to drink, but not to the point of intoxication. The dietary laws too have had the effect of teaching us moderation not only in our diet, but in everything that we do. Unlike the lower animals, man can control his appetites, and one purpose of ritual in religion is to help him learn restraint.

Our religion emphasizes that we should train ourselves systematically is discipline. Just as the musician or athlete practices self-control, so should we regulate our lives through daily discipline. That is why Judaism emphasizes the importance of performing some commandments within stipulated time schedules, and why precision and care are stressed in the fulfillment of rituals. For instance, prayers are to be recited within specified hours; the Sabbath is ushered in twenty minutes before sunset and bidden farewell with the appearance of three stars in heaven.

B: The observance of rituals also teaches gratitude. We are not permitted to overlook the day-to-day gifts that we regularly receive. The many rituals centering around the eating of food—the washing of hands, the various blessings, the grace after meals—help us to pause and reflect in gratitude for the blessing of daily bread which is so easily overlooked in time of abundance. Our gratitude is extended not only to God but to our fellow man who has made possible the food on our table.

C: The observance of rituals contributes to our maturity by instilling in us a sense of responsibility for Jewish survival. We become united in time and in space with our fellow Jews throughout the world by common observance. For example, the recitation of prayers in the original tongue helps to remind us of our bond with those who prayed in the same language throughout the centuries. We feel a sense of responsibility for them and for the values that they held so dear. The

knowledge that we are helping to keep the Jewish people together, no matter where they reside, by simultaneously observing similar rituals and ceremonies helps to prevent the
dissolution of Judaism throughout the world. To be aware
that we are seated at the *Seder* table at the same time as our
brothers in the Far East, in North Africa, or Israel, helps to
unite and solidify the Jewish people.

Similarly, when members of a community engage in ritual
acts together they create for themselves a feeling of greater
unity and strength. Their differences are minimized; their
common interests and hopes for the future are strengthened.

*   *   *

Question. Isn't religion just refined superstition or
magic?

Answer. Undoubtedly there are many naïve people who
think of religion only in terms of magic or superstition. They
feel that by praying or performing religious acts they can
force God to do their will. God is not regarded by them as
independent of man, but is expected to respond slavishly to
their wishes, for they believe that they have found the magic
formula that will force Him to act according to their wishes.
Judaism frowns upon this view of religion. That is why
Maimonides insisted that God cannot be compared to anything man can know or imagine and is therefore unpredictable
and free. He is not subject to our whims and cannot be controlled by man in any way.

In *A History of Western Morals,* Crane Brinton writes:
"There is the related distinction between magic and religion,
or 'true' religion. In magic the magician claims to have special
knowledge of the ways of the gods, or of nature, by which he
can produce results; he is a *manipulator*. In religion the

priest is the creature of the gods, at most a specially placed intermediary between the believer and the gods, but wholly dependent on the gods; he is, like the laymen from whom in many religions he is hardly distinguishable, a worshipper."

We should be careful to separate authentic religion from those superstitions that may have crept into some of our religious practices, especially during the Middle Ages. Long ago, in Biblical times, the prophets warned the people against identifying religion with witchcraft and magic. Isaiah chided those who insisted that mere fasting on the Day of Atonement could bring God's forgiveness. Amos declared that sacrifices were futile without the corresponding desire to do good.

The religious leaders in medieval times fought vigorously to divorce religion from superstition. Maimonides criticized the use of the *mezuzzah* as an amulet in warding off evil spirits. The rabbis condemned the belief in the evil eye and other superstitions as alien to genuine religion. Unfortunately, sometimes the will of the masses has been stronger than that of the great rabbis and teachers.

To condemn religion because of its abuses is comparable to condemning the practice of medicine because dishonest or disreputable practitioners exploit their patients and abuse their privileges. Intelligent people are more often than not able to distinguish the good from the bad. By studying the Jewish sources of religion they will discover that Judaism and superstition are not compatible.

The tragedy is that many ordinarily intelligent people seldom take the trouble to distinguish between true and false religion. It becomes simpler to defend one's own lack of interest in religion by pointing to its abuses. Tragically, they are contributing to its further abuse and decline by defaulting to the naïve who will continue to misinterpret religion with little opposition from those who might help restore its integrity.

*   *   *

Question. **Aren't religious people fatalists? Why, then, should a person even try to change things if he believes God is in control?**

Answer. It may appear on the surface that our religion endorses a fatalistic outlook on life, especially since many people attribute misfortune to "God's will." But our religion opposes fatalism. God does not will disease or misfortune upon innocent men. He has given men the wisdom and skill to work toward their elimination. If it were God's will to have people die of disease, then physicians and scientists would be enemies of God.

People have been perplexed with such passages in the Bible as, "God hardened Pharaoh's heart," which seems to contradict the principle of man's free will. Maimonides provides the real explanation of this passage. He said that the moral decision rests with man. At the beginning, man is free to choose the path of action he prefers. He has an equal opportunity to choose good or evil. But as soon as he makes his choice, then the freedom facing him is no longer evenly balanced; it becomes more difficult to get back on the right track; God permits him to go his own way. Thus, God permitted Pharaoh to harden his own heart.

That is what the rabbis meant when they said, "He who comes to defile himself, the way is opened for him. He who comes to purify himself is helped by God." What they are saying is that habits play an important part in our lives. We may do a thing with difficulty the first time, but soon we learn to do it more easily until it becomes an almost purely mechanical act without awareness of what we're doing. Our nervous systems have grown in the way they have been exercised. When we develop habits of impure speech, cheating, or lying, our consciousness of what we are doing becomes dulled, just as the man who swears that he never swears. This is the Biblical way of saying that God has hardened our hearts.

The following Jewish legend takes us to the heart of the Jewish view: On the second day of creation God made the angels whose nature it was to do only good. He then made the beasts which possessed only animal desires, but God was pleased with neither. He then fashioned man, a combination of angel and beast, free to follow good or evil.

*   *   *

Question. **Why is our religion usually associated with sadness?**

Answer. Every religion deals in some measure with the sad and tragic side of life, and Judaism is no exception. There are some religious ceremonies that are performed at the time of death. Much philosophical discussion centers around the mysteries of death and the hereafter. In addition, the long history of the Jewish people has been filled with experiences of tragic exile and martyrdom, and these we recall at various times in our prayers.

But Judaism is not a sad religion at all. Israel Zangwill distinguished it from other religions by calling it a "cheery creed." Much more emphasis is put on this world than the next. In opposition to some of the other ancient religions which concern themselves primarily with the preparation for life after death and hold that this life is insignificant compared to the one that follows, the Jewish sages warn us not to spend excessive effort on speculating what the future life is like because we just don't know. Since we do know more about this life, we should make the most of it, including its joys and pleasures. The Talmud reads: "When man faces his Maker he will have to give a reckoning for the joys of life that he failed to experience."

Unfortunately, many people associate their religion with sadness because their contacts with it are limited to those sad occasions. They meet the rabbi only when they have lost a member of the family. They enter the synagogue only to recite the *Kaddish,* to observe *Yahrzeit,* or to participate in the *Yiskor* service.

In reality, there are very few sad occasions in Jewish life. *Tisha B'av* is the only sad holiday because it commemorates the destruction of the First and Second Temples. Yom Kippur is solemn, but it is not a sad holiday. In ancient times betrothals were announced on the Day of Atonement. The Jew is required to make the Sabbath a happy occasion. He is forbidden to mourn on the Sabbath, nor may he fast on the Sabbath except when Yom Kippur falls on that day. He is asked to eat the finest food he can afford, to dress in his finest clothes, to use his most precious dinnerware. Joyous songs are sung around the family table on the Sabbath. Sukkot, too, is described as the "Season of Rejoicing" in our prayerbook. Pesah and Shavuot are festivals of joy and thanksgiving commemorating the gifts of freedom and the Torah, respectively.

The lifetime of the Jew is filled with occasions of joy for the celebrant, the parents, the relatives, and friends who participate in these ceremonies. If the eighth day of a newly born male child occurs on Yom Kippur, the joyous circumcision ceremony must be held then despite the solemnity of the day. True, Judaism discourages the pursuit of pleasure as a goal in life, but insists that life abounds with blessings of joy and pleasure which God wants man to taste.

*   *   *

Question. If the Bible is true, how do you account for the passages that we know today to be unscientific?

Answer. The Bible is not a book of science nor was it ever intended to be. It is rather a book that deals primarily with ethics and morality. In regard to scientific matters, we must admit that it reflects the knowledge of the age in which the authors lived. Whether the world was created in six days or over a longer period is not of major importance in our appreciation of the Bible. What is important is the belief that God's will was responsible for the creation and that the world did not just happen to come into being by mere accident, as some people claimed.

Whether the creation of man was exactly as described in the Bible or not is incidental. What is central to the understanding of the Bible is that man is unique, unlike any other of God's creatures, that he was created in the image of God with intelligence and character and with the capacity to distinguish good from evil.

It is not the factual information that concerns us, but rather the eternal truths of the Book which can help man in every generation to find direction and inspiration. A famous English clergyman responded to the problem in this way: ". . . . But the purpose of the Bible is not to further scientific discovery. Its purpose is to teach me the way to go to heaven, not the way the heavens go. In consequence, no one should marvel or think it unworthy of God that the human authors of the Bible knew no more of scientific matters than their contemporaries did and less even than what the man in the street knows today."

We, of this scientific age, are not the first to question the scientific difficulties in the Hebrew Bible. Even the deeply religious sages of the Talmud courageously reinterpreted troublesome passages in the Scriptures to meet the scientific beliefs of their day. They were willing to accept newly found knowledge as it was discovered in their generation.

In a later period Maimonides, who was thoroughly acquainted with the scientific theories of his age, sought to interpret the Bible in the light of the most recent knowledge. He, too, distinguishes between fact and truth in the Bible when he states in his *Guide for the Perplexed* that some Biblical phrases and passages should not be taken literally.

Gersonides, another medieval scholar, declares that when the language of the Torah interpreted literally is in conflict with science, the text must be interpreted so as to avoid conflict.

Judaism accepts every truth from whomever proclaims it. Those who revere the Bible need not fear that its importance will be diminished because of scientific advancement. We hail progress in science as another means of discovering the wonders of God's creation.

* * *

Question. **Why have we made heroes of those personalities in the Bible who committed immoral acts?**

Answer. The strength of the Hebrew Bible lies in its frankness and realism. It is not squeamish in reporting all the events, good and bad, in the lives of its great personalities. Those remarkable ancient editors should be commended for not deleting passages about events which displeased them.

The greatest of men lapse into sin from time to time. If they did not, there would be no need for God's direction. *People then should be judged not by isolated acts, but rather by the acts of a lifetime.* Thus, Aaron was personally responsible for the sin of the golden calf, but he fully realized what harm he had done even though he claimed that he was forced to make the idol. His role as spokesman for his brother Moses, High Priest and peacemaker, assures him an exalted role in Jewish history despite his single act of weakness.

Personalities should also be judged by the circumstances under which they commit wrongs. The rabbis do not commend Jacob for deceiving his brother, Esau, when he snatches his blessing from his father. They assert that Jacob had to pay in later years for resorting to trickery. We should, however, attempt to understand Jacob's problem. Jacob felt that he deserved his father's first blessing, since Esau had previously sold him the birthright. Furthermore, Jacob felt with his mother that the blessing would mean nothing to his crude brother, but that he alone had the responsibility to carry on the spiritual leadership where Isaac and Abraham before him had left off. To Jacob the blessing was a serious matter. Despite Jacob's act of deception, he is honored in Jewish tradition as a patriach worthy of being called Israel, after whom an entire people is named.

We also judge personalities by the way they react to their wrongdoing once they have become aware of it. Samson's sin of moral weakness may not have been as serious as David's, but nowhere do we find that Samson repented for having succumbed to the Philistine women. Samson is looked upon in Jewish history as an unfortunate person who though physically strong remains morally weak. On the other hand, though condemned by the prophet Nathan for having illegally taken Bathsheba for his wife, David confesses, "I have sinned before the Lord." A king humbles himself before the prophet! When we evaluate the life of David we do not overlook his weaknesses, but we are more impressed with his redeeming qualities. He extended his compassion even to those who wronged him; he was the most able of Israel's kings; most important of all, he is greatly revered as author of the Psalms.

*   *   *

Question. How can the Bible condone slavery if it is the great book it is claimed to be?

Answer. It is true that there is no passage in the Bible calling for the abolition of slavery. Slavery was part of the social system of the day. But we find nowhere in the Bible that slavery is sanctioned as a Law of nature or of God, as it is among the ancient Greeks. Plato in his *Republic* describes the ideal society in which slaves would serve as a defense against the enemies of the state. Aristotle, probably the greatest of ancient philosophers, also defends slavery by contending that man needs leisure in order to develop his capacities to the fullest. The slavery of the masses is justified in order to provide leisure for the select few. Greece was built on a slave economy. We are told that in Athens the ratio of slaves to free men was five to one. Among the Hebrews, however, slaves were usually those who were caught stealing and were unable to repay their debts or who voluntarily sold themselves out of poverty. Even then, they could remain slaves no longer than six years, after which they were encouraged to leave their masters.

It is clear to students of the Bible that while the elimination of slavery was not advocated by the Biblical authors, they went to great lengths to show that they were not in sympathy with the whole institution by protecting the slave's position.

1—The Bible states specifically, "Thou shalt not restore a fugitive slave unto his master." (Deut. 23:16). This law not only stands in opposition to the ancient code of Hammurabi, which demanded death for the man who harbored a slave, but also to the advocates of slavery in the American South before the Civil War. The crucial Dred Scott controversy was based on this very question of runaway slaves.

2—The master of a slave could not have complete control over him. He had to treat him humanely by recognizing his rights. "If a man smite the eye of a manservant or maidservant, and destroy it, he shall let him go free for his eye's sake." (Ex. 21:26). The owner then was expected to regard his servant as a human being and not as chattel. Brutality is not condoned by the Bible.

3—Slaves, along with their masters, were entitled to a day of Sabbath rest. Even though the heathen slave did not enjoy quite the same privileges of the Hebrew slave, he was still entitled to the seventh day of rest with the members of his family.

4—Once the slave was freed, it was the master's responsibility to help rehabilitate him so that he would not return to his former position of slavery. "And when you let him go free from you, you shall not let him go emptyhanded; you shall furnish him liberally out of your flock, out of your threshing floor, and out of your wine press; as the Lord your God has blessed you, you shall give to him." (Deut. 15:13–14).

*   *   *

Question. **Hasn't the Sabbath lost much of its meaning for the modern Jew?**

Answer. It is indeed difficult for the modern Jew, and especially one who has never seen the Sabbath observed at home, to appreciate the value of the Sabbath. It is difficult even for the experienced traditionalist to observe all of the Sabbath prohibitions that are required in the Code of Jewish Law. But one should not adopt an "all or nothing at all" attitude regarding the Sabbath since partial observance is far more desirable than no observance at all.

First of all, we should understand the continuous vitality of the Sabbath. Despite its ancient form, it has continued to fulfill the basic needs of the Jew, no matter how these needs may have changed throughout history.

In ancient times the Sabbath assured the Jew the opportunity for one day of *physical* rest. The rich were not permitted to demand uninterrupted labor of their employees. A divine mandate required them to recognize the physical needs of the laborer. In pre-modern times we find that the Sabbath served the Jew in yet another way. During the entire week he suffered humiliation and scorn; he was ostracized socially and discriminated against economically by his masters. Came the Sabbath, and the Jew was once again his own master. In his home and synagogue he was unaffected by his oppressors. The Sabbath provided him with strength and courage to endure the humiliation that he suffered for the other six days.

Today the Sabbath fulfills still another basic need for the Jew. First, it is a day of *otherness* in which he may find relief from the grind of business or professional activities which so often harass him during the week. He lives in a completely different environment for this one day. The Sabbath provides a change of pace and interest. His reading and conversation are on a more exalted level; through prayer and meditation he succeeds in replenishing himself mentally and spiritually.

In addition, the Sabbath gives modern man the opportunity to reaffirm the importance of the home and the family as the center of society. In this automotive age, when so much time is spent traveling to and from work and recreation, the home has played a less important role than it did in the past. And with all the community activities and diversions outside the home, family members often go their own way to attend their individual activities in the evening. The Sabbath helps to re-establish the centrality of the home once again by emphasizing family activity. The vitality of the home is not only indis-

pensable to a healthy society but also to the future survival of
Judaism. Unlike Christianity, which is church-centered,
Judaism is primarily home-centered, since most Jewish cere-
monies and rituals are observed not in the synagogue but in
the home. If the Sabbath ever loses its meaning for the modern
Jew, the whole future of Judaism will be imperiled.

*   *   *

Question. How can a modern Jew still believe in the
"chosenness" of Israel?

Answer. The concept of the Chosen People which is expressed in the Bible and the prayer book has been subjected
to severe criticism by non-Jews and Jews alike. On the surface
it would seem that such a concept implies that God considers
the Jews to be a superior people with special privileges and
immunities denied to the other peoples of the world. Any
Jew who still maintains this obsolete notion about the superiority of Israel is not only misinterpreting basic Judaism, but
is also performing a disservice to his people and is helping to
fan the fires of suspicion and malice toward the Jew.

The "chosenness" of Israel symbolizes a different concept.
The Jewish people by virtue of their acceptance of the
Torah at Sinai had taken upon themselves the special obligation to promote the understanding and acceptance of God's
moral law to the rest of the world.

The individual Jew looked upon himself as a member of
the Chosen People and derived from this a sense of profound
humility rather than arrogance. To think that God required
such an awesome task of him, to spread His work to the rest
of humanity, gave the Jew a feeling of responsibility for which
he often felt inadequate! But having been told that Israel
was a "kingdom of priests and a holy nation," "a light unto
the nations," "a treasured people," he was seized by this sense
of duty to serve as an instrument of the Lord.

Why should the Jew apologize for his chosenness in the realm of religion? The incontrovertible historical fact is that the world received from Israel the great ideas of ethical monotheism and prophecy, the ideals of righteousness and holiness. Has it not been established that Christianity and Mohammedanism owe their origins to Judaism? The Jew will readily admit that the Greeks were endowed with a genius for philosophy and science, that the Romans excelled in law and administration, and that the Arabs were undisputed masters in poetry and song. From all these the Jew admittedly borrowed heavily. But the Jew knew that he had a special inclination for religion and ethics which the others never achieved. He was able to take old pagan myths and spiritualize them. He imparted noble religious concepts to primitive tribal ceremonies. He knew the meaning and value of the good life even though he himself became a transgressor from time to time.

There are still strong voices among the Jews who contend that the people of Israel have not outlived their usefulness as a uniquely spiritual group, that they still have a distinct message to bring to mankind which can promote world peace. Perhaps the reconstituted land of Israel will produce new prophetic voices that will bring added hope to a divided mankind. True, there are some Jews who seek nothing more than normalcy for the state of Israel; but there are others for whom the chosenness of Israel is more than an archaic historical concept. They are impelled by the old and still vital role of the Jew.

*   *   *

Question.   Isn't one religion as good as another?

Answer.   The German author Gotthold Lessing approaches this question in the form of a parable in his play,

Nathan The Wise. A man possessed a magic ring which had the power to make its owner beloved by everyone. Each of his three sons requested their father's ring before his death. Since he loved them equally, he promised it to each one. He then sent for a famous jeweler and asked him to make two rings similar to the magic one. The father then presented each son with a ring without telling him about the rings of the other two. After his death the three sons discovered that each had a ring and asked the judge to decide who had the magic ring. The judge, finding them all alike, said, "Why decide now, we shall know when one of you becomes better liked who has the magic ring." Each brother then acted kindly and honestly as if he possessed the special ring.

The three brothers represent Christianity, Judaism, and Mohammedanism. The three religions are equal provided that their adherents act kindly and honestly, but if any one of them ceases its acts of goodness, then it will be known that theirs is not the true religion God gave to the world.

It is true that we have no other way to determine the superiority of one religion over another. All religions, if conscientiously followed, could lead its adherents to a good life; they are all true religions in the sense that they seek to bring man closer to God and to his fellow man.

However, it is natural for the Jew to regard his religion as best for himself, not because Christianity and Mohammedanism are inferior, but because he knows more about his own and feels more comfortable with it. Judaism provides emotional and intellectual stimulus for him to a greater extent than the other faiths. The same might be said for the members of other religious groups regarding their own religious beliefs.

Similarly, we prefer being members of a particular family. Most of us regard our parents as the best in the world—for us.

Our friends' parents are not expected to be as dear to us as our own. On the other hand, we respect our friends for their devotion to their families, and we expect them to regard their parents as best for them. For people to insist that theirs is the only true religion, to become involved in debate about the superiority of one's own beliefs, is as childish and as futile as an argument arising over whose parents are the best.

*   *   *

Question.   Why did the Jews reject Christianity?

Answer.   Not all Jews rejected Christianity. Most of the earliest Christians were Jews, and some of them felt there was no need to renounce their former faith because they considered Christianity to be the fulfillment of Judaism. Most Jews, however, rejected the new religion precisely because they saw in Christianity a rejection of the principles of Judaism.

(1) They could not accept the divinity of Jesus or, for that matter, of any human being. The concept of God in human form had no precedent in Jewish thought. These Jews revered the great Biblical personalities and even some of their contemporaries, but the greatest of them, including Moses, were regarded as fallible human beings.

(2) They rejected the doctrine of original sin which seemed contrary to the more hopeful and optimistic faith of Judaism.

(3) They rejected the Christian claim that the ritual commandments of the Torah had now been replaced by a mere doctrine of faith in Christ who died as an atonement for their sins; without this faith, they were told, salvation was impossible regardless of their other virtues. Even the strange concept of salvation was unacceptable to these Jews.

(4) They did not accept Christianity's faith in the resurrection of Jesus. They could not share the belief that Jesus would again return to earth to establish God's Kingdom, since

their hope for the first coming of the Messiah had not yet been realized.

(5) They were not prepared to accept the belief that the old Torah was merely a prelude or introduction to the new and more sacred covenant, which became known as the New Testament.

These new principles were for the most part formulated by Paul, who was largely responsible for the emergence of Christianity and the growing rift between the two religions. Because of his Jewish origin and background, Paul attempted to synthesize Jewish and Greco-Roman thought. After Paul, however, the Jewish influence on Christianity gradually faded as the new religion developed more elaborately. Emphasis on the role of Mary, the belief in the Trinity, the cult of the saints, and the establishment of the papacy, widened the gulf between the two religions.

Despite the many theological differences that exist between the two religions today, we find more mutual respect between Christians and Jews than at any time in the past. With the exception of the vocal minority who are still bent on converting Jews to Christianity, Christians in America are prepared to accept the fact that religious differences cannot and perhaps should not be eliminated in a democratic society. Most Jews will continue to reject those principles in Christianity that cannot be reconciled with their tradition. Most Christians will continue to reject for themselves those portions of the Hebrew Bible that deal with the ritual law and they will hold firmly to Paul's principle that faith is more essential than works. Milton Steinberg, speaking for many modernists of both faiths, sees no reason why the two religions need coalesce. "Let each be as pure and strong in its own character as it can. For the rest, there is need not for filling the gaps but for bridging them with mutual candor and understanding."

*   *   *

Question.   Isn't belief in the hereafter nothing more than a fanciful wish for a better life to come?

Answer.   Undoubtedly many people who have experienced pain and hardship during their lifetime have found consolation in the belief that all will be well with them in the life to come. Such faith has often made life tolerable for those who could not understand why misfortune befell them or their dear ones.

But the Jewish belief in a hereafter or in immortality represents more than comfort for the troubled spirit. It is rather a fundamental tenet of our religious faith.

At the same time, the Jewish view of immortality has specific unique characteristics:

A—We are advised not to speculate too much upon the after-life. When we mortals attempt to discuss the subject we are like blind men trying to understand the nature of light. It becomes a waste of time and energy to try and envisage just what the future world will be like and the benefits one will derive there. Is it not sufficient to believe that there is some form of existence beyond the grave, and that man's indestructible soul lives on? This part of us does not die with the body, but eventually returns to its original source, which is God. To imagine that we can even begin to grasp any insights into the extent of the soul's consciousness in the new life is futile. The more we speculate on such matters, the weaker our faith becomes.

B—Despite occasional rabbinic statements to the contrary, it can be stated with authority that emphasis in Judaism is centered on this life. We must not minimize this life in anticipation of the next. One of the greatest Talmudic authorities of modern times, Prof. Louis Ginsberg, wrote: "The rabbis believed in another world and often speak of reward awaiting the righteous after death. Nevertheless, the development of the religious thought of the Jew shows a marked tendency to fix the center of gravity of religion not in the thought of a world beyond but rather to foster and establish it in the actual life of man on earth. . . ." [1]

C—It is abundantly clear that Jewish belief in the after-life does not preclude one's responsibilities toward his fellow man in this world. What has been said about religion being an "opiate of the masses" cannot be applied to Jewish thinking at all. The idea that the poor can be ignored because God would eventually give them their "pie in the sky" is totally foreign to Jewish thinking. In the past, so numerous were the social obligations imposed upon the Jew to aid the poor, the aged, the orphan, the widow, the sick, and the stranger that faith in the after-life did not permit him to dull his conscience.

* * *

Question. **Do Jews still believe that the Messiah is yet to come?**

Answer. Belief in the Messiah is one of the most complicated doctrines in Judaism, for its meaning has been so widely interpreted, ranging from belief in the arrival of a golden age to faith in the advent of a great mystical figure with superhuman powers. The Talmud even records the extreme opinion of the sage Hillel who discouraged belief in the coming of the personal Messiah. The second Isaiah, on the other hand, was willing to accept King Cyrus of Persia, a non-Jew, as the Messiah for having permitted the Jews to return to their homeland. The question remains, then, what do we mean when we speak of belief in the coming of the Messiah?

[1] Ginzberg, Louis, *Students, Scholars and Saints*. New York: Meridian Books. 1958 (Paperback reprint).

The clearest meaning of what the Messiah means comes from the first Isaiah who prophesied in the eighth century B.C.E. He foresaw the advent of a great human being with rare gifts of leadership, wisdom, and piety. By virtue of these outstanding qualities he would help to bring about an era of perfect peace and universal recognition of the Lord.

This faith in an ideal future ushered in by a human Messiah partially explains why the Jews refused to accept Jesus as the Messiah. If he were the Messiah, as the Christians have contended, why does injustice, hatred, oppression, and war still prevail in the world? Christians have answered: "He will come a second time." Jews have refused to believe that he has even come the first time.

A very small segment of Jews still clings to the belief that a superhuman but less than divine Messiah will still come to perform miraculous deeds for Israel and for mankind. For this reason, a few religious extremists in Israel and the Diaspora have still not accepted the reality of Israel's independence, contending that only the Messiah can redeem the people and the land of Israel.

A still larger group continues to hope and pray for a more human type of Messiah who will possess the basic qualities described by Isaiah and will usher in the Messianic Era of world peace. This group has not denied the reality of political Zionism, and it has helped greatly to establish the modern State of Israel.

But many Jews who continue to pray for the Messiah think no longer in terms of a personal saviour. Instead, they contend that all good men who are striving and working for a better world are messiahs, there being no need to transfer the responsibility to another who may arrive at some future date. They emphasize the latter part of Isaiah's prophecy in which he foresees the Messianic Age in which the whole world,

Israel, and the nations, will be delivered. Only when men everywhere will be morally prepared to create the Messianic Age will it ultimately arrive.

An ancient parable recorded in the Talmud reflects this hope of many modern Jews. Rabbi ben Levi asked Elijah to introduce him to the Messiah. Elijah showed the rabbi the Messiah outside the gates of Rome among the poor and afflicted inhabitants. The rabbi inquired of him: "When will you come to serve mankind?" The Messiah replied: "Today." Then ben Levi remarked with astonishment: "Today? Surely that is not possible." The Messiah answered: "I am ready to come today if men will prove themselves worthy."

*   *   *

Question. **Do Jews still cling to the belief in Heaven and Hell?**

Answer. Because of the influence of Christian thinking upon Jews, it is difficult for some people to imagine that there is no specific doctrine of Heaven and Hell in Judaism. The Hebrew Scriptures contain no direct reference to this concept. *Sheol,* the grave where the dead lead a drab existence before removal to a happier sphere, has been erroneously translated as Hell by Christian scholars. *Sheol* is never described as a place of torment in the Bible, but as a region where all must one day go—the righteous and the wicked.

Only after the Jews began to live among the ancient Persians, whose religion called for belief in Heaven and Hell, did they begin to adopt this concept in their own thinking. In support of this conviction that belief in Heaven and Hell is not native to Judaism, it has been pointed out that the Hebrew words for Heaven and Hell—*Gan Eden* and *Gehenna*—are borrowed from places on earth. *Gan Eden* is the garden of Eden, when the Lord placed Adam to taste of all the earth's goodness. Likewise, *Gehenna*, which later became the term for Hell, is the name of a valley south of Jerusalem, *Ge-Ben-Hinnom,* where the wicked sacrificed their children to the god Moloch. Thus, since the Jew originally had no concept of Heaven and Hell, he had to give old names to these new and strange concepts.[1]

We can understand why the masses turned to a belief in these concepts. They frantically sought a solution for their misery and found solace in the belief that the future world would hold out brighter prospects for the righteous even if they were forced to suffer on earth. Moreover, they wanted to be convinced that the wicked oppressors would be repaid at some future time for their evil ways.

In spite of the many discussions found in the Talmud on this theme of Heaven and Hell, the Jew is not required or even encouraged to believe in it as an axiom of faith.

Some rabbis were strongly opposed even to discussing the matter. "Everyone who meddles with the following four things," says the Talmud, "it were better for him had he not come into the world: what is above, what is beneath, what is before, and what is after." Even those sages who did enjoy describing the pleasures of Heaven and the torments of Hell were usually aware that they were merely permitting their imagination to roam freely.

Few Jews today, even among the very pious, take Heaven and Hell to be actual places of pleasure or torment in the afterlife. The soul knows neither time nor space. At most, some still believe that Heaven is a state of being in which the soul of the righteous derives delight and satisfaction in a life well lived; Hell is a state of being in which the soul of the wicked is remorseful for having lived the sinful life. "If Hell is re-

---

[1] Levinthal, Israel H., *Judaism—An Analysis and Interpretation.* New York: Funk & Wagnalls, 1935.

morse, Heaven is the bliss of conscious communion with the Highest." [2]

Though Maimonides lived in the twelfth century, his view comes closest to that of the modernist. He contended that only the immature must cling to hopes of reward and fear of punishment. The reward for living virtuously, he maintained, is the good life itself. This belief, coupled with faith in im-mortality of the soul—an immortality whose nature is known only to God—is adequate for the believing Jew.

*   *   *

Question. **Isn't the religious person merely attempting to escape from the realities of life?**

Answer. Many unhappy and maladjusted people do seek escape in religion. Frightened by the insecurities of life, they seek the same kind of protection in their religion that a child receives from his parent.

Not only religion, but all aspects of culture are frequently used by some people to escape the ever-present problems of life itself. Many people find their escape in reading the type of book that excites them into picturing themselves in the roles of great heroes. For others, however, reading great litera-ture can help them cope more effectively with life's problems. Science, too, serves to compensate for the insecurity of many men; a frightened person, overwhelmed by the unpredict-ability of life, often flees to the laboratory where he feels he can master the disturbing forces of natures and thus gain much needed protection. Others find that the study of science reduces the necessity for escape.

The purpose of religion is not to provide us with escape from the problems and realities of life, but rather to make us

[2] Joseph, Morris, *Judaism As Creed and Life.* London: Routledge, Kegan Paul, Ltd., 1920.

more conscious of them. People who look merely for "peace of mind" or "peace of soul" through religion misunderstand its function. True, one of its functions is to comfort the afflicted, but it also serves to afflict the comfortable. Genuine religion does not permit one to close his eyes and say, "All's right with the world," in the presence of injustice and suffering. The prophets, who were the genuine representatives of religion, unleashed their fury against the apathetic and irresponsible privileged classes. The prophets were not escapists.

Religion also fights escapism by helping to strengthen one's attachment to society. "Do not separate thyself from the community" is a basic axiom of Judaism. Even one's enemy should not be shunned; he should be helped and ultimately converted to a friend. Our religion deems us responsible for the misdeeds of others. The Yom Kippur confessional is stated in the plural: "*We* have sinned, *we* have transgressed," to indicate that when *one* sins, it is as though *everyone* has sinned. The whole community is responsible for the failure of the individual.

Religion discourages escapism in yet another way. It demands that we tell ourselves the truth. Religion decries self-deception. It is futile to delude ourselves into thinking that we are someone else, that we can or ever should deny our identity. No matter how powerful we appear to others, we cannot hide our frailties and fears from God and from ourselves. In this area psychotherapy and religion are working toward the same goal—self-discovery. Religion fights escapism in appealing to man's courage rather than to his cowardice.

* * *

Question. Why should a modern Jew be expected to observe the ancient dietary laws now that we have such effective means of preventing disease?

Answer.   Contrary to popular opinion, the laws of Kashrut were not promulgated primarily for reasons of health. Naturally, our forefathers were concerned with preventing disease, and they probably permitted those animals to be eaten which appeared to have cleaner habits than those which were prohibited. Nevertheless, they were basically concerned with an ethical problem.

Their first goal was to enable man to become holy. To them holiness was not an impossible ideal, but something real and attainable. Taking a common ordinary act of eating and elevating it to an important religious practice was an act of holiness.

Our rabbis looked upon the eating of meat as a compromise that God made with man. Adam, it is remembered, ate only vegetation (Gen. 1:27–29). Not until the time of Noah was meat permitted (Gen. 9:1–4). However, Noah and his family were bound by certain humanitarian laws. They were prohibited from drinking blood or eating the limb torn from a live animal. Later, our rabbis set up many more intricate laws regarding the eating of meat so that before tasting flesh, the Jew would become aware that he was surrendering to human weakness. The implication is that God would prefer that we abstain from eating meat altogether, for in order to eat meat the life of an animal must be taken, but since we are not perfect and our desires cannot be thwarted completely, we must at least show control in our eating habits.[1]

This moral emphasis is further apparent in some of the specific laws of Kashrut:

1—Even permitted food must not be eaten in excess. We must curb our appetites lest we live to eat rather than eat to live.

2—Animals that may be eaten must be painlessly slaugh-

[1] Dresner, Samuel H., *The Mitzvah of Kashrut,* United Synagogue of America, 1958.

tered by a learned and reverent Jew (*Shohet*) who pronounces a blessing before taking the life of the animal.

3—The blood of the slaughtered animal must be removed before eating, since blood has been deemed a symbol of life, and this is yet another reminder that God's creation should be treated with reverence. Moreover, if blood were permitted as human food, one's conscience would eventually become dulled upon shedding the blood of human beings. Other restrictions making the eating of meat difficult, thus serving as an ethical reminder, include the separation of dishes, and the waiting period between eating meat and dairy meals.

Maimonides summarized the moral purposes of the dietary laws: They teach man self-mastery, curb his carnal desire, and cleanse him spiritually and physically. Elaborating on this opinion, Kaufman Kohler wrote: "It cannot be denied that these laws actually disciplined the medieval Jew, so that during centuries of wild dissipation he practiced sobriety and moderation." [2]

* * *

Question. How is a Jew expected to act where there is a conflict between the laws of religion and health?

Answer. There needn't be any conflict between the laws of religion and health. Judaism considers human life supreme, and in order to preserve life, any ritual law may be broken. The traditional Jew is *required* to lay aside the law when his health is in question. Not only must a person who is dangerously ill eat on the Day of Atonement, he should recite a blessing before partaking of food, since eating for him becomes a *mitzvah* (religious command). A seriously ill person who refuses a cure because it involves breaking the law should be persuaded to submit to it; indeed, continued refusal under

[2] Kohler, K., *Jewish Theology*, Riverdale Press, Cincinnati, 1943. (Reprint)

such circumstances is called "mad piety." Not only are the ill
required to depart from the law when danger to life is involved, but also those who care for them are exempt. They
may kindle a light to provide warmth or prepare food for
the sick even on the Holy Sabbath. The mandate is very clear.
Commenting on the verse, "Ye shall therefore keep my laws,
which if a man do, he shall live by them," the sages emphasize
that he shall *live* by the laws and *not die* by them. The law is
not intended to burden or punish the observant Jew, but
rather enables him to appreciate the gifts of life. Morris
Adler comments in *The World of the Talmud:* "The traditional Jew throughout the ages would not have compre-
hended such judgments as 'the curse of the Law,' 'the dead
weight of the Law,' 'the letter that killeth the spirit.' He spoke
of *'simha shel mitzvah,'* the joy of personal fulfillment that
comes from observing the Law."

The requirement to recite the daily prayers may be suspended in the event of illness. If one is too weak to stand, he
may modify his position in the interest of health. If a patient
is too weak to pray, he may meditate on the prayers in his
heart without uttering them vocally. A sick person who cannot put his mind at ease is exempt from reciting the prayers
on that particular day.

That Jewish law prefers leniency when the patient's health
is involved is unmistakably clear in Jewish tradition. One of
the underlying reasons for this liberal view may be traced to
the traditional Jewish attitude toward the human body which,
like the soul, is sacred. The soul is not regarded as imprisoned
in the body; the condition of the body largely determines the
condition of one's soul, and both come from God. "The soul
is Thine, and the body is Thy handiwork." Thus, to abuse
the body is sinful; to preserve it in a healthy state is a *mitzvah.*

*   *   *

Question. **Can one be a good Jew and a non-Zionist?**

Answer. First, we should understand what it means to be a Zionist. A Zionist is one who believes in the unity of world Jewry, the spiritual and cultural center of which is Israel. The Zionist contends that this center should serve as a home for oppressed Jews or for any Jew who chooses to settle there. In accordance with this belief, a Zionist lends his moral and financial support to the rebuilding and defense of Israel.

There are other definitions of Zionism, to be sure. Some believe that a Jew cannot be a Zionist unless he plans to settle in Israel, whether he is presently living in a free country or not. The first definition, however, is acceptable to most Jews.

Returning to the question, a Jew who severs his relationship with world Jewry not only denies a basic principle of his faith, but also reduces the chances for Jewish survival. History has shown us that those Jewish communities which chose to remain isolated eventually disappeared. Jews have for centuries claimed that their future was directly affected by the status of their brethren throughout the world. Jewish literature is filled with passages affirming the unity of Israel, without which Judaism becomes an empty shell.

World Jewry needs Israel as a spiritual center where its culture and religion can be further developed in a natural Jewish environment. New expressions of Hebrew art and literature can best be created in a Jewish homeland. These expressions will give the Jew whose home is outside of Israel renewed interest in his heritage. He will want to study Hebrew so that he can better appreciate Israel's cultural contribution. A civilization that does not continually grow to meet current needs and problems is sure to become stagnant and will eventually be ignored by the younger generation.

Zionist activity also involves a humanitarian issue. A man

does not merely fulfill a requirement of Judaism by helping the oppressed find freedom in a new land where they can live without fear and discrimination. He is, above all, performing an act of human kindness, and no man is a good Jew who is not a humanitarian.

In answer to the question, then, an anti-Zionist is still a Jew, but whether he is a Jew in the highest sense, in the eyes of the Jewish and non-Jewish community, is questionable.

Recommended Readings

Part I

Chapter 1

FOR PARENTS

Cole, Louella, *Psychology of Adolescence*. New York: Rinehart & Co., 1959.

Duvall, Evelyn Willis, *Keeping Up With Teenagers*. Public Affairs Pamphlet No. 127.

Frank, Lawrence K., and Frank, Mary, *Your Adolescent in Home and in School*. New York: Viking Press, 1956.

Gesell, Arnold, Ilg, Frances L., and Ames, Louise B., *Youth—The Years from Ten to Sixteen*. New York: Harper & Bros., 1956.

Pearson, Gerald H. J., *Adolescence & the Conflict of Generations*. New York: W. W. Norton, 1958.

FOR ADOLESCENTS

Beck, Lester F., *Human Growth*. New York: Harcourt, Brace, 1949.

Fedder, Ruth, *A Girl Grows Up*. New York: McGraw-Hill, 1939.

Jenkins, Gladys G., Bauer, W. W. and Shacter, Helen S., *Guidebook for Teenagers*. New York: Scott, Foresman, 1955.

McDermott, Irene, *Living for Young Moderns*. New York: J. B. Lippincott Co., 1956.

Menninger, William C. and others, *How to Understand the Opposite Sex*. New York: Sterling Publishing Co., 1956.

—— *How to Be a Successful Teenager*. New York: Sterling Publishing Co., 1954.

Osborne, Ernest G., *Understanding Your Parents*. New York: Association Press, 1956.

Chapter 2

Selected Chapters in:

Jersild, Arthur T., *The Psychology of Adolescence*. New York: MacMillan, 1957.

Linn, Louis & Schwartz, Leo, *Psychiatry & Religious Experience*. New York: Random House, 1958.

Remmers, H. H. & Radler, D. H., *The American Teenager*. Indianapolis: Bobbs-Merrill Co., 1957.

Chapter 3

Selected Chapters in:

Allport, Gordon W., *The Individual and His Religion*. New York: MacMillan, 1950.

Gordon, Albert I., *Jews in Suburbia*. Boston: Beacon Press, 1959.

Sklare, Marshall, *The Jews*. Glencoe, Illinois: Free Press, 1958.

FOR ADOLESCENTS—MODERN JEWISH BIOGRAPHIES

Davis, Mac, *Jews at a Glance*. New York: Hebrew Publishing Co., 1956.

Kuhn, Lois Harris, *The World of Jo Davidson*. New York: Farrar, Straus & Cudahy-Jewish Publication Society, 1958.

Leonard, Oscar, *Americans All*. New York: Behrman House, 1951.

Merriam, Eve, *The Voice of Liberty. The Story of Emma Lazarus*. New York: Farrar, Straus & Cudahy-Jewish Publication Society, 1959.

Wise, William, *Silversmith of Old New York: Meyer Meyers*. New York: Farrar, Straus and Cudahy-Jewish Publication Society, 1958.

Zeitlin, Rose, *Henrietta Szold. Record of a Life*. New York: Dial Press, 1952.

Chapter 4

Selected Chapters in:

Kohn, Jacob, *Modern Problems of Jewish Parents*. New York: Women's League of United Synagogue, 1932.

Chapter 5

FOR PARENTS

Gaer, Joseph, *The Jewish Bible For Family Reading*. New York: Yoseloff, 1956.

Golden, Judah, *The Living Talmud; The Wisdom of The Fathers*. New York: Mentor book, 1957.

Hertz, Joseph H., *The Pentateuch and Haftorahs*.

The Holy Scriptures. Jewish Publication Society.

Kaplan, Mordecai M., *Basic Values in The Jewish Religion*. New York: Jewish Reconstructionist Foundation, 1957.

Soncino Chumash and *Soncino Books of the Bible*, Soncino Press.

Selected Chapters in:

Cohon, Samuel S., *Judaism—A Way of Life*. Cincinnati: Union of American Hebrew Congregations, 1948.

FOR ADOLESCENTS

Cohen, Mortimer, *Pathways Through the Bible*. Jewish Publication Society.

Freehoff, Lillian S., *The Right Way*. New York: Union of American Hebrew Congregations, 1957.

Greenberg, Sidney, and Rothberg, Abraham, *Bar Mitzvah Companion*. New York: Behrman House, 1958.

Silverman, Althea O., *Behold My Messengers*. New York: Bloch Publishing Co., 1955.

Selected Chapters in:

Gittelsohn, Roland B., *Little Lower Than The Angels*. New York: Union of American Hebrew Congregations, 1955.

Pilchick, Ely E., *From The Beginning*. New York: Bloch Publishing Co., 1956.

Chapter 6

FOR PARENTS

Lewin, Kurt, *Bringing Up The Jewish Child*. United Synagogue Commission on Jewish Education, 1954.

Millgram, Abraham E., *Your Son's Bar Mitzvah*. United Synagogue Commission on Jewish Education, 1954.

Revitch, Eugene, *The Mental Hygiene Value of Jewish Education*. United Synagogue Commission on Jewish Education, 1954.

Segal, Abraham, *Your Daughter's Bas Mitzvah*. United Synagogue Commission on Jewish Education, 1954.

Selected Chapters in:

Lewin, Kurt, *Resolving Social Conflicts*. New York: Harper & Bros., 1948.

FOR ADOLESCENTS

Katsh, Abraham I., *Bar Mitzvah*. New York: Shengold Publishers, 1955.

Sussman, Samuel and Segal, Abraham, *A Guide for Jewish Youth*. Board of Jewish Education, Philadelphia Branch of United Synagogue, 1953.

Selected Chapters in:

Eisenberg, Azriel, *The Bar Mitzvah Treasury*. New York: Behrman House, 1952.

Chapter 7

FOR PARENTS

Duvall, Sylvanus M., *Men, Women, and Morals*. New York: Association Press, 1952.

Selected Chapters in:

Fromm, Eric, *The Art of Loving*. New York: Harper & Bros., 1956.

Kohn, Jacob, *Modern Problems of Jewish Parents*. New York: Women's League of United Synagogue, 1932.

FOR ADOLESCENTS

Duvall, Evelyn, Willis, *Facts of Life & Love For Teenagers*. New York: Association Press, 1956.

Duvall, Sylvanus M., *Before You Marry*. New York: Association Press, 1950.

Pemberton, Lois, *The Stork Didn't Bring You*. New York: Hermitage Press, 1948.

Chapter 8

FOR PARENTS

Brav, Stanley R., *Marriage & The Jewish Tradition*. New York: Philosophical Library, 1951.

Goldstein, Sidney E., *The Meaning of Marriage And The Foundations of The Family*. New York: Bloch Publishing Co., 1942.

Shoulson, Abraham B., *Marriage and Family Life*. New York: Twayne, 1959.

Selected Chapters in:

Trueblood, Elton, and Trueblood, Pauline, *The Recovery of Family Life*. New York: Harper & Bros., 1953.

FOR ADOLESCENTS

Black, Algernon D., *If I Marry Outside My Religion*. Public Affairs Pamphlet No. 204.

Selected Chapters in:

Duvall, Evelyn M., *Family Living*. New York: Macmillan, 1955.

Gittelsohn, Roland B., *Modern Jewish Problems*. Cincinnati: Union of American Hebrew Congregations, 1943.

Chapter 9

FOR PARENTS

Allport, Gordon Willard, *The Nature of Religious Prejudice*. Boston: Beacon Press, 1954.

Kagan, Henry E., *Changing The Attitude of Christian Toward Jew*. New York: Columbia University Press, 1952.

Samuel, Maurice, *The Great Hatred*. New York: Alfred A. Knopf, 1940.

Selected Chapters in:

Lewin, Kurt, *Resolving Social Conflicts*. New York: Harper & Bros., 1948.

Steinberg Milton, *Partisan Guide To The Jewish Problem*. Indianapolis: Bobbs-Merrill, 1945.

FOR ADOLESCENTS

Bettelheim, Bruno, *Overcoming Prejudice.* Science Research Associates.

Levinger, Elma Ehrlich, *Jewish Adventures in America.* New York: Bloch Publishing Co., 1954.

Selected Chapters in:
Gittelsohn, Roland B., *Modern Jewish Problems.* Cincinnati: Union of American Hebrew Congregations, 1943.

Steinberg, Milton, *The Making Of The Modern Jew.* New York: Behrman House, 1952.

Part II

FOR PARENTS

Baeck, Leo, *The Essence of Judaism.* New York: Schocken Books, Inc., 1948.

Heschel, Abraham Joshua, *Man's Quest For God.* New York: Chas. Scribner's Sons, 1954.

Jacobs, Louis, *We Have Reason to Believe.* London: Vallentine, Mitchell, 1957.

Kertzer, Morris N., *What Is A Jew?* New York: World Publishing Co., 1952.

Kohler, K., *Jewish Theology.* Cincinnati: Riverdale Press, 1943.

Levinthal, Israel H., *Judaism, An Analysis & Interpretation.* New York: Funk & Wagnalls Co., 1947.

Silver, Abba Hillel, *Where Judaism Differed.* New York: Macmillan, 1957.

FOR ADOLESCENTS

Ben-Asher, Naomi, and Leaf, Hayim, *The Junior Jewish Encyclopedia.* New York: Shengold Publishers, 1957.

Bernstein, Philip S., *What The Jews Believe.* New York: Farrar, Straus & Young, 1951.

Edidin, Ben M., *Jewish Customs & Ceremonies.* New York: Hebrew Publishing Co., 1941.

Gittelsohn, Roland B., *Little Lower Than The Angels.* New York: Union of American Hebrew Congregations, 1955.

Silverman, William B., The Still Small Voice (Vol. I) New York: Behrman House, 1955.

—— The Still Small Voice Today (Vol. II) New York: Behrman House, 1957.